MORAL CLARITY
IN THE
NUCLEAR
AGE

Also by Michael Novak:

A New Generation: American and Catholic (1964)
The Open Church (1964)
Belief and Unbelief (1965)
A Time to Build (1967)
A Theology for Radical Politics (1969)
The Experience of Nothingness (1970)
Politics: Realism and Imagination (1971)
All the Catholic People (1971)
Ascent of the Mountain, Flight of the Dove (1971)
The Rise of the Unmeltable Ethnics (1972)
Choosing Our King (1974)
The Joy of Sports (1976)
The Guns of Lattimer (1978)
The Spirit of Democratic Capitalism (1982)
Confession of a Catholic (1983)

Fiction
The Tiber Was Silver (1961)
Naked I Leave (1970)

Editor
The Experience of Marriage (1964)
American Philosophy and the Future (1967)
Capitalism and Socialism: A Theological Inquiry (1979)
Democracy and Mediating Structures: A Theological Inquiry (1980)
The Corporation: A Theological Inquiry (With John W. Cooper) (1981)

MORAL CLARITY
IN THE
NUCLEAR
AGE

Michael Novak

Thomas Nelson Publishers
Nashville • Camden • New York

Acknowledgments

The author is grateful to the following organizations:

"Moral Clarity in the Nuclear Age" is reprinted from *Catholicism in Crisis*, vol. 1, no. 4 (March 1983), and *National Review* (April 1, 1983), with the permission of the editors.

"The Geopolitical Situation" is reprinted with the permission of the Institute for Foreign Policy Analysis, Inc.

"The Bishops Speak Out" is reprinted from *National Review* (June 10, 1983), with permission.

The Scripture quotations in this publication are from the Revised Standard Version of the Bible, copyrighted 1946, 1952, © 1971, 1973.

Published in Nashville, Tennessee, by Thomas Nelson, Inc. and distributed in Canada by Lawson Falle, Ltd., Cambridge, Ontario.

Printed in the United States of America.

ISBN 0-8407-5879-0

CONTENTS

So That Our Children Will Enjoy Life,
Liberty,
and the Pursuit of Happiness

FOREWORD

Probably no document in recent decades coming from an American religious body has captivated as much public attention as the 1983 Bishops' Pastoral Letter on War and Peace. To some extent that was to be expected, of course, since Roman Catholics constitute the largest single religious group in the country. In addition, the pastoral letter may break new ground for the Bishops Conference by delving into areas of complex public policy and political controversy.

In the past, the National Conference of Catholic Bishops has tended to confine its interests and public statements mainly to spiritual concerns and issues that clearly were moral in nature. This led some to wonder if the pendulum was about to swing to the other extreme and the Bishops Conference would now imitate some of their Protestant counterparts and become overly absorbed in political activism at the expense of spiritual guidance.

But the real reason for the unprecedented interest in the pastoral letter, aside from the media's obsession with a few controversial points, is that it is a highly significant statement on the most critical political and moral issue of our time—the problem of nuclear weapons of mass destruction. However, this urgent problem also raises profound moral and spiritual questions as well—questions Christians must not ignore if they are to be faithful to their calling to be followers of Jesus Christ in today's world.

I am pleased Michael Novak's essays on this subject are being reprinted in book form. They deserve wider circulation and careful study by Christians of every background who are seeking to grapple with this complex issue. They are not only readable and logical, but seriously deal with the issues from a distinctly Christian point of view.

His essays clearly point out the major world problems and dilemmas raised by the development and deployment of weapons of mass destruction.

Mr. Novak's essays are far more than a commentary on the bishops' pastoral letter. To be sure, they will be a useful introduction to that complex document, but beyond that, they present a brilliant discussion of the whole question of morality and nuclear strategy. Of course, not everyone will agree with his perspective or every detail of his argument, but his views cannot be ignored by anyone who claims to be dealing seriously with this issue. His awareness of the dangers our world faces and his burden to bring the light of Christian teaching to these dangers come through on every page.

The essays in this volume are important for

another reason, however. Novak rightly points out that the basic problems of our time—and of our individual lives, I might add—are fundamentally spiritual in nature. For too long modern man has tried in vain to solve his problems without God, but when humanity seeks to live apart from its Creator and His unchanging moral law, the result is always chaos. Those of us who are Christians are convinced the ultimate answer to the problems we face is found only in Jesus Christ, who freely offers forgiveness and new life to all who turn to Him in repentance and faith.

May these essays confront us afresh with that truth and lead us to seek God's wisdom and help in every area of our lives, both as individuals and as a nation.

—BILLY GRAHAM
August 1983

INTRODUCTION

When I was at college, more than thirty years ago, *The New Yorker* magazine astonished the journalistic world by devoting the whole of one issue to a single essay. It was an essay on what exactly happened, that day in August 1945, when the *Enola Gay*, an Air Force B-29, let drop an atomic bomb on Hiroshima with an explosive power of 20,000 tons of TNT. Some had sensed it immediately, for others the knowledge came gradually—that we had entered a new age. At *The New Yorker* the gravity of the event was recognized by a decision undertaken, one must suppose, with trepidation, and humility. It is now generally agreed that the symbolic deference paid to the event at Hiroshima, by a weekly magazine of urbane renown, was both a spiritual acknowledgment of the transcendent magnitude of the event, and an invitation to analytical meditation on its implications.

In February 1983 I reflected that an event of corresponding magnitude was upon us. It isn't something that has exploded, in the manner of a bomb bursting in air. But its philosophical radioactivity is far-reaching and, at the margin, quite as deadly. It is an analytical evolution of which Hiroshima is the godfather. Namely, the notion that the explosive might of the nuclear bomb is the operative datum in the formation of morally defensible public policy. That development, i.e., the suggestion that public policy should proceed on the understanding that no use of nuclear weapons is morally defensible, not even the threat of their use as a deterrent, is nothing less than an eructation in civilized thought, putting, as it does, the protraction of biological life as the first goal of modern man. The new doctrine comes at us from many sides, in many voices, in varied tempos, with many allurements heavily moral in tone.

Now although there has been with us, for almost as long as the event at Hiroshima, a movement that asks for unilateral disarmament, we have tended to view that movement as merely another expression of the fundamentalist pacifism with which the social order has been familiar for many generations. And there are those who, while they have not called explicitly for unilateral nuclear disarmament, have set forth positions that, if they were put into effect, would almost certainly bring on such disarmament, even as the logic of the wheel is to turn.

We address ourselves here not to the professional appeasers, not to those who defend the policies of the Soviet Union as a matter of course, even as they tend to oppose our own policies as a matter of course. The current division is among Americans who find themselves staring, stupefied, at the evolving positions of their nextdoor neighbors. There are, suddenly, very bright men and women around town, individualistic in their intellectual habits, thoroughly and happily habituated to the exercise of their own freedoms, who are suddenly saying that (a) we must not own nuclear weapons, if (b) the idea is inherent in the ownership of the weapons that there are circumstances in which they would be used. The arguments are made with great force, and are growing in popularity, even among citizens who associate themselves instinctively with the conventional axioms of American idealism, such as we celebrate on the Fourth of July, and proclaim when we sing the national anthem.

No other declaration brought home so clearly the dimensions of the philosophical assault on right thought as the second draft of the pastoral letter prepared in 1982 for the voting of the American Catholic bishops at their May (1983) conference. It was by no means merely the episcopal authority of American bishops that gave prominence to the working document. It was, rather, the phenomenon of such men, whose moral pedigrees, national and ethnic inclinations, and historical attitudes, have all along suggested that in congregation they would take exactly opposite positions from those with which they were increasingly associated, that abruptly awakened many Americans to what is going on. That serious people believe the correct thing to do, at this point in the nuclear age, which is also the age of Gulag, is, well: to disarm.

National Review is not a "Catholic" publication.

(Indeed its editor, although he is most emphatically a Catholic, has from time to time been criticized by some Catholics who have reprimanded as ventures in indocility some of his positions.) When, twenty years ago, *National Review* inaugurated a religious section we asked Dr. Will Herberg, a prominent Jewish theologian, to administer it. Among those who have held the position since Will Herberg's death have been two Protestant scholars. Today, our religion editor is Michael Novak, a Catholic scholar who has administered that portfolio for more than three years.

In 1982, under his own aegis, Michael Novak, the author of many learned books, an activist for human rights at the United Nations, a backer of George McGovern in 1972, the author of *The Spirit of Democratic Capitalism*, set out to analyze the arguments put together by a committee of Catholic bishops against the maintenance of a nuclear arsenal. In doing so he consulted many scholars, many of them Protestant or Jewish, some of them agnostic. What came out of this prodigious effort (in form, an open letter to the American Catholic bishops) is a document that, in virtue of rigorous thought, plain language, and eloquent moral reasoning, cannot fail to achieve ethical consequence. After the bishops brought together their third draft, and met in Chicago, Mr. Novak wrote a second essay, summarizing the movement from the second to the final draft.

This book, which contains both of Mr. Novak's essays together with the appropriate narrative joinerwork, makes specific references to papal utterances. But there is no point at which it leans marginally on distinctively Catholic preconceptions or loyalties. Pope John Paul II is quoted not because Catholics believe that, in carefully restricted circumstances, he speaks infallibly. He is in any case quoted, to begin with, not when proclaiming doctrine ex cathedra. He is quoted as a great religious leader. So also are quoted, with profound respect, such authors as C. S. Lewis and Reinhold Niebuhr. There are as many references to the Old, as to the New Testament. Indeed no agnostic, reading this document, would feel in any sense excommunicated by an exclusivist Christian, let alone Catholic, denominationalism. Although the author of the document believes in God, in the divinity of Christ, and in the inspired provenance of the Bible, it is not expected that any reader of this book should need to do so in order to sense the document's gravity, marvel at its moral lucidity, and experience, finally, the serenity of exposure to thoughts marshaled so harmoniously. It is a document for the age, and we should be grateful that it appears now in book form. Without disparaging the importance of those bishops who have energized the antinuclear movement, I like to think that what will prove historically most important about their own pastoral letter, is that it engendered Michael Novak's *Moral Clarity in the Nuclear Age.*

—WILLIAM F. BUCKLEY, JR.

AUTHOR'S PREFACE

From its inception in 1981, it became apparent that the draft letter of the U.S. Catholic bishops on nuclear war would be issued during a tempestuous period. The Soviet SS-20s, which had been put in place since 1979, were striking terror in the hearts of Europeans. This event reminded many Americans of the terror *they* had been living under since the early 1950s, American cities having been targeted by Soviet ICBMs. Fear is a healthy emotion, but morally speaking, everything depends on what is done with that fear.

Early in 1982, a group of Catholic laymen and laywomen decided to prepare a draft statement of their own. While it eventually fell to me to write the three drafts of the document, more than two hundred other persons, experts in various areas, offered corrections, emendations, new arguments, and other suggestions. Finally, the third draft appeared in March 1983, in a new journal *Catholicism in Crisis* (P.O. Box 495, Notre Dame, Indiana 46556). Almost simultaneously, recognizing the significance of such a statement for all

16

citizens, Christian or not, William F. Buckley, Jr., in an unprecedented manner, devoted an entire issue of *National Review* (150 East 35th Street, New York, New York 10016) to this document. To both journals, requests for reprints and letters streamed in—more than eighteen thousand— from persons of every religious and political point of view. The document struck a profound moral chord.

Every U.S. bishop received the document, and some expressed gratitude. An influential few received its successive drafts from January through March. For reasons discussed in Chapter 3, the bishops' letter in its final draft (May 1983) reached rather similar positions, more so than in their earlier drafts. The main influence in this direction seems to have been strong argument from certain bishops, buttressed by the advice of the Vatican on January 18–19. "Moral Clarity in the Nuclear Age" was translated into German almost immediately, first for private and then for public distribution, and is credited with affecting the statement by the Catholic bishops of West Germany.

"Moral Clarity" was signed by more than one hundred prominent Catholic lay persons and has been widely read by church leaders of all other denominations. It was placed in *The Congressional Record* both by U.S. Representative Vin Weber (R-Minn.) and by Senator Robert W. Kasten, Jr. (R-Wis.), and was widely cited during congressional debates, by Democrats and Republicans alike.

Since religious leaders of many denominations

have now called for wide and full debate, I hope this modest initiative, undertaken by Catholic lay persons, together with bishops and clergy, sheds light on matters no similar effort has addressed. Whatever its faults, which belong to the author, I hope it proves valuable in strengthening the West, so that war may be prevented. As we go to press, Andrei Sakharov's brave letter from within the Soviet Union has just been published in *Foreign Affairs*. Citizens, he tells us,

> . . . have the right to control their national leaders' decision-making in matters on which the fate of the world depends. But we don't even know how, or by whom, the decision to invade Afghanistan was made! People in our country do not have even a fraction of the information about events in the world and in their own country which the citizens of the West have at their disposal. The opportunity to criticize the policy of one's national leaders in matters of war and peace as you do freely is, in our country, entirely absent. Not only critical statements but those merely factual in nature, made on even much less important questions, often entail arrest and a long sentence of confinement of psychiatric prison.[1]

The freedom we possess is precious. Noting, as Sakharov urges us to note, the effective role of Soviet propaganda in the media of the West, we need to think clearly about the global strategic situation in all its components, as factually and coldly as we can. Where "Moral Clarity" is

18

wrong, let others set it right. Free societies reach consensus through considering rival arguments, learning from each.

I thank Ralph McInerny of *Catholicism in Crisis;* William F. Buckley, Jr., of *National Review;* Robert L. Pfaltzgraff, Jr., and Jacquelyn K. Davis of the Institute for Foreign Policy Analysis; Larry Stone of Thomas Nelson, Inc., for allowing me to express the fruits of my own reflection—and all those many who helped to shape these views.

PART 1

They shall beat their swords into plowshares,
  and their spears into pruning hooks;
nation shall not lift up sword against nation,
  neither shall they learn war any more.
                    —Isaiah 2:4

Beat your plowshares into swords,
  and your pruning hooks into spears;
let the weak say, "I am a warrior."
                    —Joel 3:10

The following text appeared in Catholicism in Crisis *(P.O. Box 495, Notre Dame, Indiana 46556) in March 1983, vol. 1, no. 4. The text reprinted in* National Review *(April 1, 1983) represents a slightly earlier version, edited so as to reduce the number and length of the footnotes. The full body of the notes is preserved here.*

Chapter 1

MORAL CLARITY IN THE NUCLEAR AGE

A Letter from Catholic Clergy and Laity

Although in recent times, as in earlier times, there has been a tendency to use the expression "the church" to mean chiefly its ordained leaders, the clergy, the church in fact consists of the entire people of God, including those laymen and laywomen who participate in "the saving mission of the church." As the Second Vatican Council puts it:

> Every layman should openly reveal to [his pastors] his needs and desires with that freedom and confidence which befits a son of God and a brother in Christ. An individual layman, by reason of the knowledge, competence, or outstanding ability which he may enjoy, is permitted and sometimes even obliged to express his opinion on things which concern the good of the Church. When occasions arise, let this be done through the agencies set up by the Church for this purpose. Let it always be done in truth, in courage, and in prudence, with reverence and charity toward those who by reason of their sacred office represent the person of Christ (*Lumen Gentium*, #37).

In recent years, many laymen, laywomen and clergy have awaited the early drafts of a pastoral letter from the U.S. bishops on morality in nuclear matters. Both the first and second drafts which have appeared have awakened many questions. Rather than merely react to flawed portions of the two early drafts—with which many bishops are not yet satisfied—it seemed wiser to attempt a constructive statement of our own reasoned moral views. The task is immensely difficult. No more than our bishops do we expect complete unanimity. Emulating their example, we are moved by our responsibilities to the gospel of Jesus Christ and to our vocations as Christians in the world. We hope that this constructive act will be useful to our bishops, and we make it public in accord with their express desire that the complex issues involved be treated to extensive and reasoned debate.

For nearly the whole of our adult lifetimes, since the first use of atomic power, and since the passing of its secrets into the hands of the USSR, we have all lived under the shadow of new and terrible weapons. Descriptions of the horrible devastation which might be wrought upon the entire world through these weapons have been set before the public not only in scientific testimony but also in popular novels and movies. For more than thirty years, a primary moral imperative placed upon governments and peoples has been to assure that these weapons shall never be unjustly used.

The technology upon which these weapons are based is sufficiently simple that its secrets have now become dispersed throughout the world. Knowledge is good in itself; so is human liberty. We can scarcely wish that these secrets had never been learned. Moreover, it is virtually impossible that, once discovered, they can wholly be repressed or permanently banished from this earth. The moral imperative that they never be unjustly used, therefore, will retain its full force for the foreseeable future.

Yet it must be observed immediately that such weapons have two quite different uses. The most obvious use is through their explosion in warfare. The more subtle use is through intimidation, since powers which possess them exercise over others who do not a threat beside which conventional armed defenses pale. While the use of nuclear weapons in the first sense is most to be guarded against, use in the second sense also constitutes a grave danger to justice, liberty, and peace. The moral imperative mentioned above applies to both uses.

More than once in our lifetime, superior nuclear force has obliged weaker nations either to surrender (Japan) or to abandon projects in which they were engaged (USSR in Cuba) or otherwise to moderate their intentions and actions. The possession of nuclear weapons seems also to have moderated actions which might in other times have led to confrontation by force of conventional arms. In this sense, while nuclear weapons constitute a grave threat to justice, liberty, and peace, their possession has also had pacific effects.

From biblical times, the human race has often been warned that God might will or permit its destruction. When Cain slew Abel, he prefigured the possibility of a threat to all the progeny of Adam and Eve, including himself, for by the same passion he might have slain not only his brother but also his parents and finally himself. In the story of Noah, the Bible instructs us in an image of the destruction of the whole world by flood, and warns us of God's threat to destroy all the world by fire. Sodom, Gomorrah, and other cities were utterly destroyed in vivid biblical warning, as was the Temple of Jerusalem. To live under threat of flood, fire, glacier, plague, pestilence, war and destruction is not novel for an imagination attuned to biblical history. The destruction of Carthage, the leveling of the glories of Greece and Rome, and the coming night of barbarism inspired St. Augustine to oppose secular millenarianism and a false sense of catastrophe, as he penned *The City of God*. The ruin of civilization is not a theme new to our time, nor is the theme of the destruction of all things living. Since Jewish and Christian conscience has long been steeled by contemplation of the fragility of this world and the overpowering sovereignty of God, our generation should not separate itself too dramatically from all others. The prophecies in the Book of Revelation exceed even the horrors of the twentieth century.

In fulfilling the moral imperative to prevent unjust uses of nuclear weapons, therefore, Christian citizens must exercise clear and sustained thought. Any flight of reason into panic must be quietly resisted, and every flight into illusion curbed. Both for good and for ill, the "mobilization of the masses" has frequently characterized life in this century. Neither slogans nor cold fear is a suitable substitute for prudent judgment. Questions of this magnitude cannot be left to experts, governmental or ecclesiastical, but must be prayerfully and lucidly reflected upon by all citizens. Only a broadly supported, carefully reasoned public policy, sustained over decades, meets the imperative laid upon all of us. Strong majorities must grasp and nourish such a policy.

For this reason, we Catholic citizens welcome the effort of the National Conference of Catholic Bishops in the United States, and the bishops of various conferences in Europe and elsewhere, to draft pastoral letters on nuclear arms. The bishops have a right and duty to express the truth of the Gospels entrusted to them and to restate the Catholic tradition for our time. On these matters, they, and only they, in their vocation as teachers, have full authority with respect to the Gospels and the Catholic faith.

According to the teaching of Jacques Maritain and Etienne Gilson, there are three spheres of Gospel teaching in human life.[1] The first concerns the life of the spirit, human life in the light of eternity. The second concerns those areas of the social order on which the Gospels and Catholic teaching directly impinge and in which they are necessarily enmeshed—such areas as are addressed in the social encyclicals of the popes, for example. The third concerns the area of worldly interpretation of social reality and fact, tactical and strategic judgment oriented to results in the concrete world of history, choice among various permissible means, practical detail and, in general, questions of prudential judgment.

While in all three spheres every member of the church may have important witness to contribute, there is an ordinary differentiation of functions and authority. In the first of these spheres, the teaching of the bishops is clear and supreme when in conformity with that of the Holy Father and the whole college of bishops. In the second, the teaching of the bishops and popes is necessary and fruitful, although more engaged with matters fraught with ambiguity and danger of error. In the third, the focus of Catholic teaching normally passes from the hands of the bishops and popes to the concrete moral reasoning of individual Catholics responsible for fulfilling their vocations in the world. This is because in the world of contingency and action, church leaders cannot summarize all concrete possibilities, but must enunciate religious ideals and moral principles and demand that lay persons apply them to concrete situations prudently and prayerfully. In this third sphere, the God of the Last Judgment will not be satisfied by a claim that a Christian followed the general authority of his bishop or of anyone else; each will be judged by what he or she did in the light of his or her own concrete moral reasoning in particular cases. From such personal responsibility, there will be no escape in the encompassing light of Judgment.

It is in this third sphere that we associate ourselves in the task of Christian moral reasoning, reflecting on the realities of nuclear weapons in our time. We are conscious of the presence of God. It is His judgment we fear. "The fear of the LORD is the beginning of wisdom" (Prov. 9:10). Being faithful to the teachings of the Gospel and of the Catholic tradition, including the recent teachings of the Second Vatican Council, the popes, and the bishops, we propose to deal as clearly and as conscientiously as we can with the prudential matters of the third sphere. We speak for no others but ourselves. The matters with which we wrestle are, in the nature of the case, full of ambiguity, complex in their chains of reasoning, dependent upon difficult judgments of fact at every step. Other Christians of good will are certain to make quite different judgments at any ten or twelve places in the argument. So it always is in complex judgments of fact. We are certain only that we have tried to be faithful to biblical realism: both to the Gospels and the Catholic tradition, and to a realistic assessment of matters of fact and rational principle. We welcome argument, since it is by argument that we have arrived where we are, and by argument that we hope to learn. Among ourselves, we also have differences. Nonetheless, we have found it possible to offer what follows as a public and moral policy which we as Catholics support.

Peace in the World Today: Catholic Perspectives

The Catholic tradition on war and peace is long and complex: it reaches from the Old Testament and from the beginning of the New, from the slaughter of the innocents at the birth of Christ to the baptism of the Roman centurion, from the practice of the early church to recent statements by Pope John Paul II. Its development cannot be sketched in a straight line. It seldom gives a simple answer to complex questions. It speaks through many voices. It has produced multiple forms of religious witness.

We rely upon *The Pastoral Constitution on the Church in the Modern World* and on *The Decree on the Apostolate of the Laity* of Vatican II as the most authoritative recent statements on the question of nuclear weapons and on the role of the laity. We note that *The Pastoral Constitution* carefully differentiated in its own teaching between those elements "of permanent value" and others of "only a transitory one." It said that future "interpreters must bear in mind . . . the changeable circumstances which the subject matter, by its very nature, involves."[2] In this spirit, we are mindful of the indispensable, central role of accurate discrimination and sound prudential judgment.

We note also that Vatican II did not speak of nuclear weapons as such, but of "scientific weapons."[3] We understand this more general concept to be essential, since developments in rocketry, computers, and explosives since 1945 have given even "conventional" weapons awesome destructive power at great distances and with amazing accuracy. Because of their power, many of the novel conventional weapons seem to fall under the same moral strictures as do nuclear weapons, in terms of proportionality and discrimination in targeting. Indeed, the larger conventional weapons now exceed in their destructive power the smaller nuclear weapons. If one cannot distinguish between such weapons on the scale of sheer physical power, nonetheless, the divide between conventional and nuclear explosives is a critical boundary.

The Pastoral Constitution bids us to read the "signs of the times." We note three vital factors, in particular. The first is recorded in *The Pastoral Constitution* itself:

> Insofar as men are sinful, the threat of war hangs over them, and hang over them it will until the return of Christ. . . . In spite of the fact that recent wars have wrought physical and moral havoc on our world, conflicts still produce their devastating effect day by day somewhere in the world.[4]

The second comes from that Constitution's definition of peace:

> This peace cannot be obtained on earth unless personal values are safeguarded and men freely and trustingly share with one another the riches of their inner spirits and their talents.[5]

This is not the peace of totalitarianism. It is the peace of liberty and justice. The third vital factor is that considerations of the need to avoid nuclear war

> . . . compel us to undertake an evaluation of war with an entirely new attitude.[6]

It is a moral imperative to deter not only nuclear war but all war. Yet the very act of nuclear deterrence has its own novel characteristics, involving new ways of thinking about intention, threat, use, means and ends, and lesser evils. "An entirely new attitude" is required on some of these matters.

At the center of the Catholic teaching on war and peace is, first, the sovereignty of God and, second, the dignity of the human person. The perennial sinfulness of humans makes the threat of war perennial; the longing of humans to be true to the image of God within them makes perennial the longing for peace. Directly to take innocent human life is a prerogative only of the sovereign God, the Author of life. To defend the dignity of human life is both the motive force of peace and the just cause of war. When an unjust aggressor injures human dignity, to stand aside is a form of complicity and collusion. To resist an unjust aggressor with proportionate means is demanded by justice. Thus, human dignity is the cause both of just peace and of just war. As there are wars which are unjust, so also there is peace which is unjust.

It is sometimes held that there are on these questions plural traditions in the Catholic church, one addressed to Catholics and another addressed to the pluralistic public, one evangelical and the other based on natural law, one committed to pacifism and the other committed to the tradition of just-war reasoning. But there is not one teaching for initiates, another for the uninitiated; not one teaching for the perfect, another for the imperfect. In the matter of celibacy and marriage there may be two vocations in the church, yet one vision of a common faith. So in matters of war and peace there is more than one vocation, yet one common teaching about justice in war and in peace. One common set of precepts, many different counsels; one life of charity, many different vocations: this is our vision.

Peace and the Kingdom

Athough God has always promised His people peace and rest, the paradoxical nature of these promises is ever present in the Bible. "Not as the world gives do I give [peace]," Jesus said (John 14:27). Again: "I have not come to bring peace, but a sword" (Matt. 10:34). And, admonishing Peter in Gethsemane, Jesus said: "Put your sword back into its place; for all who take the sword will perish by the sword. Do you think that I cannot appeal to my Father, and he will at once send me more than twelve legions of angels? But how then should the scriptures be fulfilled, that it must be so?" (Matt. 26:52–54).

In the Old Testament, God is often portrayed as One who leads His people into battle, whose power helps them to prevail, who avenges wrongs done to them by their enemies. Paradoxically, Gideon says "God is peace," and the blessing of the Lord on Israel includes this, that "the LORD lift up his countenance upon you, and give you peace" (see Num. 6:23–27). Ezekiel speaks for Yahweh: "I will make a covenant of peace with them; it shall be an everlasting covenant with them . . ." (Ezek. 37:26). Yet as sin persists, so does war. False prophets "have healed the wound of my people lightly. . ." (Jer. 6:14). Peace would have come, had humans not persisted in sin: "O that you had hearkened to my commandments! Then your peace would have been like a river, and your righteousness like the waves of the sea" (Is. 48:18). Only in the time of full righteousness and no more sin, the people "shall beat their swords into plowshares, and their spears into pruning hooks; nation shall not lift up sword against nation, neither shall they learn war any more" (Is. 2:4).

Although Jesus came as the Prince of Peace, inaugurating a kingdom of peace, He was a man of sorrows, bloodily slain on the cross. He called His disciples to share in self-sacrifice. His vision of this world was no vision of the easy triumph of justice and light. On the contrary, the vision of Jesus is a divisive force in history, dividing even families, a two-edged sword "piercing to the division of soul and spirit, of joints and marrow, and discerning the thoughts and intentions of the heart" (Heb. 4:12). It will divide believer from infidel. It will trouble individuals, like the rich young man (see Matt. 19:16–26), and in time divide the nations. In this world Jesus does not promise peace. When Jesus speaks of peace, it is not as the absence of war between nations, or as an end to terror and lies, but, rather, as a form of knowing and being in union with God (see John 17:3), a peace which the world cannot give (see John 14:27). It is worth noting that no one in the New Testament thinks of telling the Roman centurions to give up their military careers—neither Jesus (see Matt. 8:5–13), nor John the Baptist (see Luke 3:14), nor St. Paul (see Acts 22:25).

In being condemned to a cruel death (see Gal. 3:13), Jesus did not defend Himself against unjust treatment and assaults upon His human dignity. He followed here not His will, but His Father's, offering a redemptive sacrifice for all. His gentleness under torment, His nonviolence, and His forgiveness of His killers have led some to choose in imitation of Him nonviolence as a way of life, both in their persons and in public policy. We recognize this choice, but believe it to be a misreading both of the Scripture and of virtually the entire Catholic tradition. We sharply distinguish between pacifism as a personal commitment, implicating only a person who is not a public figure responsible for the lives of others, and pacifism as a public policy, compromising many who are not pacifists and endangering the very possibility of pacifism itself. It is not justice if the human race as a whole or in part is heaped with indignities, spat upon, publicly humiliated, and destroyed, as Jesus was. It is not moral to permit the human race so to endure the injustice of the passion and death of Christ. Many classic arguments against pacifism as a Christian vocation have been offered in Christian history. Closest to our own time, the arguments of Reinhold Niebuhr and C. S. Lewis may be cited. While following closely the paradoxical language of the Scriptures and the Catholic tradition, and choosing against pacifism for ourselves, we honor the liberty of others to choose differently, and in particular the calling of the clergy not to take up arms.

Kingdom and History

With Pope John Paul II we hold:

Christian optimism based on the glorious cross of Christ and the outpouring of the Holy Spirit is no excuse for self-deception. For Christians, peace on earth is always a challenge because of the presence of sin in man's heart.

Although Christians put all their best energies into preventing war or stopping it, they do not deceive themselves about their ability to cause peace to triumph, nor about the effect of their efforts to this end. They therefore concern themselves with all human initiatives in favor of peace and very often take part in them. But they regard them with realism and humility. One could almost say that they relativize them in two senses: They relate them both to the self-deception of humanity and to God's saving plan.[7]

History is open; therefore, one must always say that "Peace is possible." On the other hand, we heed Pope John Paul II, who observes "that in this world a totally and permanently peaceful human society is unfortunately a utopia, and that ideologies that hold up that prospect as easily attainable are based on hopes that cannot be realized, whatever the reason behind them."[8]

History is full of ambiguities, contingencies, and complex patterns of fact. No two people perceive world affairs in identical fashion. Interpretations even of the simplest events radically diverge. In this respect, we cherish the wisdom of *The Pastoral Constitution:*

> Very often their Christian vision will suggest a certain solution in some given situation. Yet it happens rather frequently, and legitimately so, that some of the faithful, with no less sincerity, will see the problem quite differently. Now if one or the other of the proposed solutions is too easily associated with the message of the Gospel, they ought to remember that in those cases no one is permitted to identify the authority of the church exclusively with his own opinion. Let them, then, try to guide each other by sincere dialogue in a spirit of mutual charity and with anxious interest above all in the common good.[9]

The Moral Choices for the Kingdom

From some early Christians through Dorothy Day and Martin Luther King, Jr., some Christians—joining others like Leo Tolstoy, Mahatma Gandhi, and Norman Thomas—have held that any use of military force is immoral. Yet we observe that military and police power has been necessary from time immemorial to preserve civilized societies—and pacifists themselves—against únjust aggression and brutal violation of rights. As a set of practical methods, nonviolent techniques have preeminence for nonpacifists as well as pacifists. They are, after all, the stuff of diplomacy and statecraft, within which adversaries observe civil discourse and amenities of many sorts. Athough a full discussion of these issues would take us too far afield, we observe that there are important distinctions to be made between force and violence, between non-violence and pacifism, and between the power and the authority of the state. For example, nonpacifists prefer nonviolence to violence, respect for legitimate authority to naked state power, and legitimate uses of force to violent acts. Deterrence itself is a form of nonviolence, a legitimate use of force, based upon legitimate authority.

While some Christian communities, such as the Mennonites, the Quakers and the Church of the Brethren, make the refusal of military service an obligation for their members, the Catholic church has not done so—indeed, has afforded many arguments, biblical and theological, moral, and political, against pacifism. In this world of sin and threat of war, for every pacifist who refuses to take up arms, some other citizen, who would also prefer to live in peace, must take his place. Nonetheless, in the full liberty of an open church, nonviolent witness through a conscientious refusal of military service has been honored in the Catholic tradition. Recognizing this liberty of conscience, we nonetheless argue against the pacifist option, as did C. S. Lewis:

> Only liberal societies tolerate Pacifists. In the liberal society, the number of Pacifists will either be large enough to cripple the state as a belligerent, or not. If not, you have done nothing. If it is large enough, then

you have handed over the state which does tolerate
Pacifists to its totalitarian neighbour who does not.
Pacifism of this kind is taking the straight road to a
world in which there will be no Pacifists.[10]

Thus widespread pacifism in churches and universities during the 1930s helped convince Hitler and the
Japanese that the West lacked the resolve to defend
itself, and encouraged them to launch World War II.

The pacifist refuses to restrain with proportionate
force an aggressor who is injuring the innocent. By
contrast, St. Augustine understood the command of
love to demand a just defense of the innocent. This is
because St. Augustine understood that the world of
history is in part evil, and that action to restrain evil is
an essential component of justice. While some Christians stress the fact that the "New Kingdom" has
already come with Jesus, others, like Augustine, stress
the continuing power of sin and the complex texture of
social ambiguity. War, for example, may arise from
human sinfulness, but it may also afford a tragic
remedy for sin in political society. (It was in this spirit
that we observed above that the possession of nuclear
weapons has had both threatening and moderating
effects during the past twenty-five years.) Moreover, if
love demands the defense of others (such that a failure
to defend them can be a sin), both love and justice also
command self-defense. Peace is sometimes unjust;
war is sometimes morally imperative. In clarifying
such paradoxes, the traditional just-war teaching has
stood the tests of time. Many who claim to reject it do,
nonetheless, invoke its criteria; as, for example, in
judging nuclear weapons immoral (for lack of propor-

tionality and lack of discrimination), in defending wars of liberation like those against Somoza and the Shah, and in opposing the U.S. presence in South Vietnam.

The essence of just-war theory lies in the conviction that wars are wrong and to be avoided, except under quite stringent conditions. These are seven in number: (1) Only a *competent authority* may declare a war for the common good and in the interests of the public order. (2) War must be inspired by a *just cause:* such as to defend against aggression, to protect innocent life and human rights from real and certain injury and to resist tyranny. (3) A *right intention* must guide the purpose, means, conduct, and aims of war in the light of the "just cause." Violence may be chosen only (4) *as a last resort,* when all peaceful methods of negotiation have failed, and (5) with *probability of success*—so that irrational resort to force is not mandated in the name of justice. The nature of the war itself must manifest (6) *proportionality:* the damage to be inflicted and the cost incurred must not constitute a greater evil than the evil to be avoided. (7) *Just means* which are *both discriminate* and *proportional* must be employed. This means that: (a) *discrimination* between combatants and civilians, while not easy to observe under modern conditions, must be maintained in every act of war; (b) the *proportionality* of each act of war derives from its indirect, collateral, and long-term effects. It will be noted that common sense criticism of wars and the conduct of wars usually fall under one of these headings.

There are some gaps in just-war theory today, since new conditions have raised new questions. Among these may be mentioned the following: (a) Does any band of idealists or cynics that takes up arms in the name of a "just cause" constitute a competent authority to launch a just war? (b) Under what circumstances, if any, are acts of terrorism (that is, violent acts directed at persons, property, or public order), for whatever motives, whether revolutionary or absurdist or other, justified? (c) Considering the current literature of instruction in the conduct of guerrilla warfare, the training of terrorists, and the techniques of espionage and subversion, what light can be shed by "just-war theory" on existing practices in widespread underground wars? (d) According to just-war theory, is a "cold war" of espionage and counter-espionage to be preferred to a "hot war" of conventional conflict, as a means of self-defense; and, if so, according to what standards of behavor? (e) Under the "paradoxes of deterrence" (to be discussed below), does the traditional teaching on "intention" have to be refined and stated more precisely? (f) If it may be concluded that a particular totalitarian regime is evil in a special way—as was the case with National Socialism under Adolf Hitler, at least from the time of the death camps in 1941—do other nations accrue moral responsibilities, in the name of justice, for what happens *within* those regimes? What responsibility have citizens of one nation to be keepers of the human rights of those of another? These are only a few of the unanswered questions of our day.

War and Peace Today

Because of the unparalleled power of nuclear weapons, it is easy to be deflected from reasoned discourse.

When one has listened to eminent scientists and physicians detail the horrors of the worst imaginable case of nuclear destruction, one is driven to recall the lessons of Christian faith about the precariousness of all human life, the approaching end of history, the perennial wickedness and obdurateness of the human race, and the total sovereignty of God. Nuclear weapons have changed our world but have not altered the fundamentals of the Jewish-Christian vision. In the biblical era, only about 50 million human beings, widely separated from each other, lived on earth. Under ancient conditions of communications, those who lived in a village, a town, a region, or even a country believed they knew "the whole world," and did not know they inhabited a tiny planet spinning in space. For them, the destruction of their whole world could descend in one violent sacking, pillage, and leveling—as, more than once, the heads of infants in Israel were dashed against stones; and as Moscow, Kiev, and Warsaw fell to Mongol invaders in horrors still not forgotten. Images of horrible plague and destruction often arose in medieval times. Not even our fears are as novel as we think. This is the context in which Pope John Paul II said at Hiroshima: "In the past it was possible to destroy a village, a town, a region, even a country. Now it is the whole planet that has come under threat."[11] Today, nuclear weapons add new dimensions of scale and time, through prolonged radioactivity. These new possibilities made two questions most insistent: Can nuclear war be prevented? If so, which strategies and tactics, and which principles of human behavior, are most likely to succeed in preventing it? The first question involves a principle:

41

we must seek to prevent nuclear war. The second, while also involving principles, is ultimately a question for prudential judgment.

The "New Moment"

There is a widespread, well-organized, and well-financed "peace movement" in several free countries today, particularly in those about to make decisions for their future defense against superior nuclear forces now arrayed against them: West Germany, the Netherlands, Denmark, Belgium and the United Kingdom. (France is militarily independent of NATO and has its own deterrent; its peace movement is far less visible.) There is also a well-organized peace movement in many cities in the U.S. Some find the public discussion here and abroad "unprecedented in its scope and depth." Democratic societies entrust such matters to public discussion; that is one reason they are worth defending. Democracy itself depends upon the civility, reasonableness, and wisdom of the discussion.

Political peace has always been precarious, as when statesmen imply fragility in such phrases as "the balance of power." An overall balance of power, always shifting, does not *guarantee* peace. Yet experience has shown that the capacity to retaliate in kind has prevented some weapons systems from being used, even when peace is breached—witness chemical weapons in World War II. But deterrence has never been wisely thought of as a "safe and stable" system, except by comparison with other proposed alternatives. Today a spiritual sea change does threaten deterrence. Since 1945, the 400 million persons of the

North Atlantic Alliance have enjoyed liberty and prosperity unparalleled in human history. Changes in material conditions also unleashed new possibilities for spiritual fulfillment. This great transformation in life has been sudden and profound. Children can scarcely know the almost wholly different conditions under which their parents entered upon life during the depression and wartime. The horrors and deprivations of forty years ago are unknown to a majority of those now living. Consequently, unrealistic and utopian expectations find fertile soil. Deterrence is sometimes judged against ideals, not against recent history. There is a danger that history may once again repeat itself, not only in Europe but elsewhere. Preserving peace and defending justice are political tasks, and politics, while always ambiguous and imperfect, is the instrument of natural law for the protection of the weak and the innocent. Constitutional law, democratic procedures and political processes are far from perfect, but they are noble in their dependence upon civil discourse, persuasion, and realistic judgment about the less than perfect.

To be sure, it is tragic that so much treasure has had to be spent on arms since 1945. The postwar world might have been different. Moreover, if one compares the crude atomic bomb of 1945 and its primitive delivery system with the weaponry thirty-seven years later to be found in the arsenals of the U.S. and the USSR, one sees that the "arms race" means not only treasure spent but conditions transformed. This is true even though the total money spent on nuclear weapons and their technology has been a very small fraction of U.S. economic resources. Expenditures on the research and production of nuclear weapons by the United States since 1945 have been estimated to be less than $400 billion, about $12 billion per year. In fiscal year 1983, U.S. expenditures on nuclear weapons constitute nine per cent of the military budget, 2.9 per cent of the entire federal budget, and about 0.6 per cent of GNP.[12] Compared to conventional arms, nuclear arms are vastly less expensive.

Under the terms of the treaties ending World War II, the United States has chiefly been charged with the defense, not simply of its own interests, but of Western Europe and Japan as well. After the war, all Western nations virtually disarmed. Even in face of a massive Soviet build-up since 1965—the most massive in peacetime history—the defense budget of 1981, as a percentage of GNP, was for Belgium, 3.3; Britain, 5.4; Canada, 1.7; Denmark, 2.5; France, 4.1; Germany, 4.3; Greece, 5.7; Italy, 2.5; Japan, 0.9; Luxembourg, 1.2; Netherlands, 3.4; Norway, 3.3; Portugal, 3.8; Spain, 1.9; Turkey, 4.5; U.S., 6.1.[13] (It is estimated that the Soviet Union spends, for its military alone, not counting the military KGB, between 11 and 12 per cent.)[14] These considerations suggest two conclusions. First, the percentage of national resources spent on arms by Western allies is low. Second, the percentage of national resources spent on *nuclear* arms, in the case of the U.S., is ten times lower. Thus, when in 1976, the Holy See condemned the arms race as a danger, an act of aggression against the poor, and a folly which does not provide the security it promises, the Holy See could not reasonably be interpreted as asking the Western allies to spend much less than they are. The reason for poverty in the world is not adequate defense. Furthermore, efforts to supplant reliance on nuclear weaponry with reliance on conventional weaponry are bound to raise military costs dramatically, since conventional weapons are far more expensive.

While we cannot speak for the "arms race" of Third World countries or in the Soviet Union, we do note that the percentage of world gross economic product being spent on arms has declined during every year since 1967. In 1978, the last year for which figures are available, the world spent 5.4 per cent of its gross economic product on arms, down from 6.7 per cent a decade earlier. In 1978, this amounted to $480 billion.[15] Since virtually all nations of the world are welfare states to some degree or another, it must be noted that government expenditures alone for health and welfare, not counting expenditures by private citizens on their own behalf, amounted to several times more than military expenditures. In the United States, for example, the percentage of the *federal* budget spent on health and welfare programs of various sorts during 1982 was 51 per cent, and on the defense budget 26 per cent.[16] This does not include human services provided by state and local governments and by private agencies of every sort. Since the United States bears the free world's heaviest defense burden, comparisons of percentages of human services expenditures to military expenditures in West Germany, the United Kingdom, and other nations are even more favorable. In the free nations, moneys from all sources spent on health, education, welfare and other human purposes exceed moneys spent on weapons by a factor of about 20 to 1.

It is, nonetheless, true that lower spending on defense would be advantageous to all. Since government spending which creates deficits has implications for inflation and unemployment, every reduction in pressure on government budgets may have creative effects throughout the economy. For many reasons, we favor the minimum amount of defense spending consistent with moral obligations to defend the innocent with just means. We recognize that moral means may be more costly than less moral means, as conventional deterrence may be more expensive than nuclear deterrence, but we accept this as the price of moral behavior.

To say no to nuclear war is both a necessary and a complex task, especially since *saying* no doesn't make it so. It is also a task full of paradox, and demands new ways of thinking. It is a task demanding perseverance from one generation to another. It is a task exquisitely dependent upon cool-headedness and the force of reason, a task made difficult by outbursts of passion, hyperbole, flagrant accusation, and misleading assertion. In denouncing the relations between the United States and the USSR for being based upon a balance of nuclear power, some critics fail to imagine the consequences of losing a war to tyrannical powers. Some also fail to imagine the consequences of attempting a balance of conventional power. First, the history of modern Europe is not reassuring about balances of conventional power. Second, world leaders do not seem by their behavior to fear conventional wars (of which there have been more than sixty-seven since World War II) as they fear nuclear conflict. Third, currently the conventional military arms of the Soviet

Union sufficiently outnumber those of Western Europe as to create an imbalance, whose rectification would require immediate, sustained and heavy military expenses by Western nations. A political leader seeking to solicit those expenses from voters might not be successful, and might not win support from the churches, universities, and the press. In short, an alternative to the nuclear balance is easier to talk about than to realize. Further, it is one-sided to speak of "psychological damage" done to ordinary people, especially the young, by the nuclear balance without comparing it to the "psychological damage" which would be caused by heavier taxes and conscription for conventional forces, on the one hand, and by intimidation under "Finlandization," on the other hand. Appeasement, too, causes "psychological damage." It is also extreme to contrast the "billions readily spent for destructive instruments"—seventeen billion dollars were spent in the U.S. in 1982 on strategic forces[17]—with "pitched battles" being waged in the U.S. Congress "about a fraction of this amount for the homeless, the hungry, and the helpless." Moneys allocated by Congress for housing assistance, food stamps, Medicaid, Medicare and other forms of welfare vastly exceed moneys allocated for nuclear arms. Although one might wish that cuts in spending on nuclear weapons would go to the homeless, the hungry, and the helpless, the second draft of the Pastoral Letter of the U.S. Catholic Bishops (November 1982) prudently observes: "Rejection of some forms of nuclear deterrence might therefore require a willingness to pay higher costs to develop conventional forces. Leaders and peoples of other nations might also have to accept higher cost for their own defense if the United States government were to withdraw any threat to use nuclear weapons first."[18] Saying no to nuclear weapons may, therefore, impose a greater burden on the poor than at present.

Religious Leadership and Public Debate

Religious leaders who wish to influence public policy by influencing public opinion owe a special debt to democratic states, and incur an obligation to defend them against those who would destroy them. "Rulers must be supported and enlightened by a public opinion that encourages them or, where necessary, expresses disapproval," Pope John Paul II says, thus preferring societies in which the public may express disapproval of their leaders.[19] Is it just to defend such societies with nuclear weapons? Some would "build a barrier against the concept of nuclear war." But a parchment barrier will not prevent nuclear war. As even God's commandments have frequently been disobeyed, so also a nuclear war may be waged by sinful men. Since this possibility cannot be excluded, it does not seem wrong for the potential victims of nuclear war to give some thought to "surviving" it. Is it a necessary assumption that any one use of any one type of nuclear weapon will result almost at once in the explosion of every nuclear weapon? History is full of surprises and sudden turns. What seems most probable often does not occur. Prudent leaders must, therefore, consider other possible eventualities.

It is possible that one step into nuclear warfare will escalate outside human control to total expenditure of every nuclear weapon. But this is not the only possibility. Moral reflection requires the moralist to face other eventualities. Today, these possibilities are shaped by two great concrete realities: the actual nature of the Soviet Union and the actual nature of the United States and other Western democracies. The problem of saying no to nuclear war is not abstract; it is concretely directed most of all to Moscow, to Washington, and to European capitals. Actual decisions about existing and forthcoming nuclear weapons are made by real persons in specific political and geographic locations. Moral thinking about nuclear war must be concrete, as well as abstract.

The Concrete Moral Context

In deciding ethical questions in political matters it is wise procedure to seek first a clear grasp of realities, interests, and powers. This attained, one then wisely asks: "What ought we to do?" and appeals to all one's resources of vision and principle. Virtually all arguments about the prevention of nuclear war hinge on judgments concerning the nature of the Soviet Union and its nuclear forces. In 1968, the U.S. had a larger number of nuclear warheads, a greater total throwweight, and a larger and more varied number of delivery systems, than did the Soviet Union. In an effort to promote arms control, Defense Secretary McNamara froze the strategic bomber fleet at 600 aircraft, froze the number of land-based missiles at 1,054, and froze the maximum number of nuclear submarines at 41. Subsequently, by 1982 the total throwweight of U.S. nuclear arsenals has been reduced by more than one-half, and warheads have been reduced in number and in size.[20] Emphasis has been placed upon smaller, more accurate warheads, in order to meet just-war criteria of proportionality and discrimination, and in order to avoid entrapment in a strategy of Mutual Assured Destruction. (We ourselves judge that this shift away from MAD is morally correct despite the fact that MAD affords conceptual simplicity and lower costs.) Since 1968, no new delivery system for the U.S. land-based missiles has been built, no new bomber has been built, and both the ICBM missiles (1,052) and the B-52s (316) are entering obsolescence.

Since 1968, by contrast, the Soviets have developed the number, power, variety, and accuracy of their delivery systems and warheads. As Secretary Harold Brown said: "When we build, they build. When we stop building, they build." The U.S. did try a freeze, for fourteen years. The trend lines of Soviet forces kept mounting, while those of U.S. forces either fell or rose more slowly or have now become subject to public pressure for a freeze. The Soviets have now developed a strategic triad with nuclear weapons on aircraft and in submarines. Their land-based missiles outnumber ours by a third, and are more modern, larger, and more powerful.[21] Although some critics of U.S. policy fear that the U.S. may by 1990 develop a "first-strike" capability against Soviet land-based missiles—an intention denied by U.S. officials—the Soviets already possess such a capability.[22] Their land-based missiles are sufficient in number and power to deliver at least two warheads on each of the 1,052 American silos, while still retaining a large number of warheads and delivery systems for a second strike. If it is wrong for the U.S. to have a first-strike capability, it would seem to be wrong to acquiesce in the Soviets having one.

Some citizens are inclined to stress the possibilities of negotiation, agreement, neighborly coexistence, and perhaps even ultimate friendship with the Soviets. Pointing out that now friendly nations like Germany and Japan were not long ago our foes, they correctly say that in world affairs there are no permanent enemies. They believe that taking risks, making first steps, and launching initiatives will draw the Soviet leaders into amicable, or at least nonhostile, relations. Since the days of Lenin, the Soviets have supported frequent "peace offensives." Surely, some citizens conclude, peace is better than war, agreement better than conflict, amity better than struggle. Much depends on how cynical Soviet leaders are. If their purpose is the eventual destruction of democratic societies, feigned friendship may suit them now. On the other hand, if they intend to become a nation like other nations, committed to live and to let live, respectful mutuality may be possible. Among these and other possibilities, how would we judge the purposes and character of the leadership of the Soviet Union? That is the factual question on which subsequent ethical judgment turns. Naiveté in this judgment, on the one hand, or excessive cynicism, on the other, would undercut moral correctness in later judgments. For it is not moral to place trust in a liar, nor is it moral, from erroneous hardness of heart, to refuse trust. Judgment about the leadership of the Soviet Union must be carefully developed, beginning with their own view of themselves and their strategies for war, or else further moral judgment is flawed. This is another instance of the crucial role played by prudence.

In assessing the purposes and character of the Soviet

leaders, it is crucial to observe three facts. First, the number of relevant decisionmakers is very small (fourteen in the Politburo), and their means of attaining power and of holding power are far from regular, systematic, open, and under public control. Much jockeying goes on; there have been many murders, executions, disappearances, and obliterations from the historical record ("nonpersons") among them. Second, the ideology of Marxism-Leninism which legitimates their role in history, their authority, and their morality operates as a check upon their behavior. Even for those who do not believe this ideology in their hearts, ideological deviation may swiftly become a source of vulnerability to their positions and their lives. Third, the culture of centuries of Russian experience, including xenophobia and a sense of inferiority, affects their understanding of the role of the Russian people in history. Observers properly debate what comparative weights to assign to each of these three characteristics: organizational struggle; the ideology of Marxism-Leninism; and Russian experience and culture. All three factors bear on the Soviet sense of security and historical destiny. All three must be soberly considered. Whether one entertains prospects of friendship or coexistence or struggle with such leaders is much affected by such assessment. How one weighs the moral value of Soviet words and deeds is also affected by one's judgment about their cultural world. Words spoken and deeds done have full significance only in such contexts. How to interpret their significance within one's own context is quite a different matter.

The record of arms control negotiations during the

past hundred years has been, for the most part, a record of deception on the part of the cynically ambitious and of self-deception on the part of those who thought peace might be bought cheap.[23] The course of negotiations of other nations with the Soviet Union on nonaggression and noninterference pacts, and concerning treaties on chemical and biological warfare and the like, has always required unusual amounts of vigilance against betrayal. Marxist-Leninist ideology rejects "bourgeois formalism," including promises and signed agreements; Soviet practice in observing treaties, while sometimes good, is selective. Furthermore, to demand on-the-ground verifiability of Soviet arms is to demand a sweeping change within the structure of Soviet society. Despite all this, negotiations are both necessary and useful. But signed agreements by Soviet leaders cannot be understood by prudent persons as deterrents to any course of action Soviet leaders choose to take when they choose to take it. Parchment barriers have seldom restrained players of Realpolitik.

In 1968, Defense Secretary McNamara judged that U.S. strategic forces were both superior to Soviet forces and at a point of sufficiency for the deterrence of any possible Soviet attack. For this reason, he instituted the freeze mentioned above. Secretary McNamara's judgment was that the Soviets would build up their forces until they reached parity. By 1972, with the signing of SALT I, leaders on both sides claimed that parity had been reached. Since 1974, the Soviets have added two new generations of delivery systems and warheads, with others in development. This includes missiles of unprecedented size and throwweight for the strategic services, and large, swift missiles for the European theater as well.[24] In a sense, the nuclear initiative has passed into Soviet hands.

As for the United States, military budgets in constant 1972 dollars remained relatively level from 1962 to 1982, and expenditures for nuclear weapons as a percentage of the military budget and in constant 1972 dollars have also remained remarkably level.[25] From 1968 until 1976, virtually every presidential campaign and many congressional campaigns were conducted on the pledge to cut military spending. As a proportion of GNP, military spending went from 9 per cent in 1960 to 5 per cent in 1980. As a proportion of the federal budget, military spending during the same period went from 44 per cent to 23 per cent. Beginning under President Carter, then raised again under President Reagan, the military budget (in actual outlays) has now been slated to rise, in real terms, at 7 per cent per year, reaching about 6.3 per cent of GNP and 32.4 per cent of the projected federal budget for 1984. Unlike other nations, the United States is charged not solely with its own defense but with that of Western Europe and Japan. It is estimated that the maintenance of 303,000 troops in Europe costs the defense budget $133 billion yearly, compared to the expenditure (in 1981) of $16.7 billion on all nuclear forces together.[26] U.S. strategic bombers, under the McNamara freeze, have been reduced from 600 to 315. The number of land-based ICBMs remains at 1,052. The number of nuclear submarines remains at 32, of which only half are on station at any one time. Military hardware inexorably becomes obsolete and less reliable with age. Even without expanding capacity, the replacement of weapons systems every ten or fifteen years is required. Such hardware, therefore, has a time factor: a preponderance (almost two-thirds) of U.S. delivery systems are older than ten years, while a preponderance (more than two-thirds) of the Soviet delivery systems are less than six years old.[27] Technology, of course, does not stand still, so new generations of weapons have new potential. For U.S. forces, such changes have been generally in the direction of greater accuracy and smaller warheads, subject to control of greater precision.

U.S. military strategy is defensive in configuration. This fact is clearest in conventional weaponry. Neither U.S. nor NATO forces are equipped for offensive use, not in numbers of tanks, nor in numbers of fighters, bombers, or support vehicles. No attempt has been made to match Soviet forces on the Western front tank for tank, artillery piece for artillery piece, aircraft for aircraft. To equalize the numbers of U.S. forces with Soviet forces in Western Europe would require raising the number of NATO fighter planes and interceptors from 3,100 to the 8,600 in the Warsaw Pact forces. To equalize tanks would require raising the northern NATO number of 10,500 to the Warsaw Pact number of 27,300. The Soviet all-ocean navy now numbers 2,429 ships, the U.S. Navy 514.[28] The task of equalizing all forces is not necessary for two reasons. First, the NATO configuration is defensive, the Soviet offensive. Second, U.S. forces are believed to hold a technological edge, which, however, has diminished over the years.

It has long been recognized that democracies are inferior to dictatorships in their capacities to mobilize armies during peacetime. Free voters are reluctant to bear expenses not widely seen to be essential; they discern many social needs of greater moment and value. Free economies seem to thrive on production for peace rather than for military purposes, as the Japanese, West German, and other economies demonstrate. The ideology of the West does not require the destruction of socialism, but the ideology of Marxism-Leninism does teach a law of history according to which socialism must replace capitalism. A part of this law is encapsulated in "the Brezhnev Doctrine" that nations, once Socialist, may never be permitted to return to an earlier stage in history. Such cultural and political discrepancies are also part of the present reality.

The Imperative of Deterrence

It is not necessary to decide the argument whether Soviet forces, nuclear and conventional, are now superior to U.S. forces, whether in Europe or worldwide. Forces superior in number are not necessarily superior in other respects. More important for forces committed to defense is the simpler question of sufficiency for deterrence of aggression. Superiority is not essential. Sufficiency is. Moreover, sufficiency to deter aggression is a moral imperative of the right to self-defense and the duty to defend the innocent from unjust aggression. This includes the defense of good citizens living now under totalitarian regimes who, as Solzhenitsyn reminds us, would be left by our failure without any hope whatever.

This is the concrete context within which the moral standing of doctrines of deterrence arises. The overriding moral imperative is to deter the use of nuclear weapons, both their explosive use and their political use to intimidate the free. To fulfill this imperative, prolonged social sacrifices and resoluteness of public will are indispensable. To weaken this will is immoral, since a public unwilling to meet these sacrifices fails in its moral duty. That duty is purely defensive.

Some hold that it is not enough to deter aggression. One must also attempt to bring about changes in the potential aggressor, especially by appeals to self-interest in avoiding mutual destruction, by negotiations, by cultural exchanges, by trade, and, in a word, by peaceful and friendly pursuits. With these arguments we are in full accord, when and insofar as the potential aggressor shows himself by deeds to be a mutual partner. Adolf Hitler, however, both betrayed and was betrayed by Joseph Stalin. Not all states seek relations of mutuality. In affairs of state, Aristotle once observed, one must be satisfied with a tincture of virtue. Reinhold Niebuhr in *Moral Man and Immoral Society* showed with several reasons why this is so. Just conduct can, however, be morally demanded of states, and exacted by the force of arms.

An adequate morality of conduct between states, therefore, must take account of the varying moral conduct of different states, including outlaw states whose only moral law is their own aggrandizement. Such states have appeared, and do appear, in history. Knowledge about how such states act is pivotal.

In this context, moral clarity in a nuclear age raises exceedingly difficult questions. A major complexity is this. The possession of Soviet nuclear arms on the borders of the West has political uses far beyond material considerations like potential physical destruction; this point has been well stressed by German Catholics. Since nuclear weapons have a political as well as an explosive use, deterrence of both uses demands a sufficiency of threat. The only known path to this sufficiency is a corresponding threat of destruction to a potential aggressor's industrial base or else of its warmaking capacity. The first alternative is called "countervalue," the second "counterforce." The moral problem posed by countervalue strategies is that they hold noncombatants in urban areas hostage. The moral problem posed by counterforce strategies is that they awaken possibilities of a hair-trigger response to perceived threats. The countervalue strategies require much less accuracy, fewer warheads and delivery systems, and much less expenditure. The counterforce strategies require far greater technological sophistication, numbers, precision, and prior intelligence. It must be said that both strategies make one sad, except by comparison with the only current alternative. That alternative is to fail in the duty of defending the innocent, by having no deterrent at all. Such a dilemma, like the Fall, ought not to have existed, but when it does exist, actions to prevent evil are not bad but good. On its face, it would seem that countervalue strategies are less to be approved, by the just-war criteria of proportionality and indiscriminate taking of innocent life. Countervalue strategies give rise to the terror of Mutual Assured Destruction. On the other hand, some support them because they seem to afford less risk of miscalculation and cost less money. Furthermore, some regimes are such that they do not shrink from using Western principles to confound Western strategies, deliberately emplacing offensive weaponry amidst civilian targets.

It is clear that the complexities of nuclear deterrence change the meaning of *intention* and *threat* as these words are usually used in moral discourse. Those who intend to prevent the use of nuclear weapons by maintaining a system of deterrence in readiness for use do *intend* to use such weapons, but only in order *not* to use them, and do *threaten* to use them, but only in order to *deter* their use. That this is not mere rationalization is shown by the fact that several generations of nuclear weapons systems have become obsolete and been retired, without ever having been used. These are considered the successful and moral systems. In the same way, deterrence is judged to be successful insofar as nuclear war does not occur.

That a human system like deterrence is not infallible, is not foolproof, and does not convey full safety and security, goes without saying. In the world of contingent matters of fact, no system is. That one might devoutly wish for some other alternative also goes without saying. Contemplation of the horror of a breakdown in deterrence, through either the outbreak of nuclear hostilities or the intimidation of innocent peoples, leads some to seek a way out of this dilemma by putting the best possible face upon the enemy to be deterred. But this is to deny the premise from which the dilemma arises in the first place. Were the Soviet Union a benign nation, even a nation like Japan and Germany, a nation like others, the need for deterrence would by now have much diminished or disappeared.

The U.S. has no deterrent in place against any other power. The reality of the Soviet Union is the linchpin of the dilemma.

But the moral dilemma remains. No choice before U.S. leaders is wholly satisfactory. To abandon deterrence is to neglect the duty to defend the innocent, to preserve the Constitution and the republic, and to keep safe the very idea of political liberty. No president by his oath of office can so act, nor can a moral people.

We must, then, confront anew the moral hazards of deterrence. The fundamental moral principle at stake is to make the moral choice which occasions the fewer evil consequences. To abandon deterrence occasions the greatest evil, for it entails endangering that liberty which is more precious than life itself. Free societies are an indispensable social condition of free moral life and the preservation of human rights. That is why for the signers of the Declaration of Independence (and for millions before and since) liberty is worth the pledge of life, fortune, and sacred honor. Insofar as deterrence succeeds, no evil is committed and the worst evils—whether of destruction under nuclear war or of abandoning the duty to preserve liberty—are avoided. It is the fundamental moral intention of those who embrace deterrence that it should succeed in preventing these worse evils. Those who say that deterrence may fail are, of course, correct. But they do not, and cannot, show that the abandonment of deterrence will succeed either in preventing nuclear devastation or in preserving liberty. Their claim to a superior morality is, therefore, flawed in a fundamental respect.

An example may illustrate this. Had Japan had the

capacity in 1945 to strike Sacramento and Portland as Hiroshima and Nagasaki were struck, one may doubt that President Truman would have ordered the flight of *Enola Gay*. In that case, a bloody amphibious assault on the Japanese mainland may have had to ensue, with far greater devastation and loss of life than actually occurred. Two points arise from this illustration. Without justifying the decision of President Truman, the first highlights the uses of deterrence from the point of view of the Japanese. The second highlights the awful destructive force even of modern conventional warfare. It was perhaps for this reason that the Second Vatican Council spoke of "modern scientific weapons" rather than explicitly of nuclear weapons.

Some find the moral flaw in deterrence in the choice of an evil means to attain a good end, calling this "consequentialism." They admit that the end of preventing nuclear war is good. But they hold it evil actually to intend to use any deterrent force lacking proportionality and moral discrimination in order to attain this end. This formulation contains, we judge, two flaws. First, the appropriate moral principle is not the relation of means to ends but the choice of a moral act which prevents greater evil. Clearly, it is a more moral choice and occasions lesser evil to hold a deterrent intention than it is to allow nuclear attack. Second, the nature of the intention in deterrence is different from intention in ordinary moral action. There is a paradox in its nature, such that the word *intention* is clearly being used equivocally.

It is true that on entering the arena of public policy and prudential judgment, moral actors who make public policy are bound primarily by the ethic of consequences rather than by the ethic of intentions. ("The road to hell is paved with good intentions.") Further, existing alternatives in a world of sin often present policy makers no alternative that is purely good, and oblige moral actors to choose the course that occasions the least evils. Nonetheless, the quality of moral intentions deserves moral scrutiny. Alas, the word *intention* (like *threat*) has many meanings. Since many moral issues cluster here, some detail is necessary.

In the carrying of a firearm, (a) a policeman, (b) a burglar, and (c) a murderer each has a different intention with respect to using the firearm. The policeman intends deterrence but no actual use unless governed by justice and the disciplines of his profession; the burglar intends only a threatening and conditioned use, outside justice; the murderer intends not a conditional but a willful use. These three are only a few of the many senses of *intention* and *threat*. The intention in deterrence, for example, is analogous to case (a), not to (b), and certainly not to (c). In nuclear matters, we would further distinguish between a fundamental, secondary, and architectonic intention. Each of these must also be treated in turn.

The fundamental moral intention in nuclear deterrence is never to have to use the deterrent force. That this is in fact so is shown by the honorable discharge of military officers, after their term of duty expires, who have succeeded in their fundamental intention. Besides this fundamental intention, however, deterrence requires by its nature a secondary intention. For the physical, material weapon is by itself no deterrent without the engagement of intellect and will on the part of the entire public which called it into being. It is also no deterrent if it fails to meet and to halt the will, intellect, and social organization of the particular opposing regime. A people which would be judged incapable of willing to use the deterrent would tempt an adversary to call its bluff. Thus, a secondary intention cannot be separated from deterrence. Without that secondary intention, distinct from the fundamental intention, a deterrent is no longer a deterrent but only an inert weapon backed up by a public lie.

As a counter to this, some might argue that the Soviet Union could never be sure whether a weapon held in readiness were backed by the secondary intention to use it. Given Soviet ideology about the perfidy of capitalist powers, however, Soviet leaders would be obliged to assume the worst. Arguing the casuistry of truth-telling may indeed permit leaders of one nation to allow the leaders of another, who have no title to know the truth, to be self-deceived. But probes and tests of real intentions cannot be ruled out. In nuclear matters, such uncertainty willfully created would seem to constitute immoral behavior.

The word *intention* has yet a third sense, beyond the two subjective intentions we have so far discussed. The Catholic moral tradition holds that human acts have objective intentionality apart from subjective dispositions. In order to construct and to maintain a nuclear deterrent force, a democratic society must generate a complex, highly rational, socially organized, objective intentionality. Citizens through their representatives vote funds for it; research and production are organized, elaborate systems of communication and command are maintained. The architectonic of objective political intention suffuses the entire process. This already is a sustained intention of a crucial sort. To be sure, many individuals must also be committed to their tasks to suffuse this objective intentionality with appropriate subjective dispositions. The latter are indispensable. But a society which possesses a deterrent also has an organized objective intention. In the case of the United States, individuals add to this objective intention subjective intentions which are both fundamental—that the deterrent succeed in never being used—and secondary—that the deterrent be held in readiness for use. To say that a nation may possess a deterrent but may not intend to use it is fulfilled by the fundamental intention. Not so by the objective intention and the secondary intention. To condemn weapons held in readiness (and the secondary intention to use them) is to frustrate deterrence and to invite a host of greater evils.

Moral clarity in a nuclear age requires that governments not willfully allow certain kinds of miscalculation to arise in the minds of other governments. While not every capability or intention or option needs to be—or should be—revealed, a basic and clear set of understandings is necessary. This requirement rules out bellicose threats as it rules out mere bluff. Public statements about nuclear policy must, therefore, be unambiguous and reasoned, restrained and understated. Leaders have sometimes erred in this matter. Communications links between adversaries should be swift, clear, unthreatening, and unambiguous, especially during times of stress. The record of the last thirty-seven years shows that this is difficult but possible.

A dilemma arises when some say that countervalue strategies are immoral in subtance but preferable on grounds of economy and sufficiency; but that counterforce strategies, more moral in substance, are immoral because more dangerous. A similar dilemma arises when some say that making nuclear weapons smaller and more precise, so as to approximate the force of larger conventional weapons, thus reducing the moral problem of proportionality and indiscrimination, makes the use of nuclear weapons more thinkable and so should be avoided. If the use of both sorts of nuclear weapons is to be deterred, total reliance on one alone is likely to enlarge the options and temptations of an aggressor.

Similarly, some critics condemn the attainment by the U.S. of a first-strike capability, while ignoring the fact that the Soviets already have, or very shortly will have, this capacity with respect to U.S. land-based delivery systems. By first-strike capability is meant the capacity to destroy the opponent's delivery systems before they can be called into use. This the United States does not have, and has no plans to attain. The one hundred MX missiles requested by Presidents Reagan and Carter (who requested 200) cannot possibly wipe out all Soviet land-based missiles. Since two warheads on each silo are believed to be required, the 1,398 Soviet land-based delivery systems cannot be threatened by the MX, for it would be suicide to strike some without destroying all. Meanwhile the existing 1,052 American silos *are* vulnerable to the multiple-warheads of a fraction of the Soviet missile force. Since U.S. B-52s are not likely to penetrate Soviet defenses, a first strike by the Soviets may leave only submarine-launched missiles under U.S. command. To launch these would guarantee a second strike on U.S. cities. Given these capacities, the Soviets could, even without a first strike, hold U.S. forces immobilized and in checkmate, freeing Soviet conventional forces from restraint. Nuclear weapons do not have to be fired in order to exact surrender.

The reasons why the U.S. maintains a strategic triad—land-based, airborne, and submarine-borne delivery systems—are two: first to reduce the temptation of a simple first strike and, second, to prevent the president of the United States from facing only a single option, the command to destroy Soviet cities. Such an option would be suicidal for American cities. No president can be fairly placed in that position.

In short, given the nature of the Soviet leadership, its ideology, and its political culture, and recognizing the configuration of its own nuclear forces, we see no completely satisfactory position: neither abandonment of the deterrent, nor a deterrent strategy based upon counterforce, nor a deterrent based upon countervalue. Among these, we judge the best of the ambiguous but morally good options to reside in a combination of counterforce and countervalue deterrence. We uphold the fundamental intention of deterrence that no nuclear weapon ever be used. We uphold the secondary intention of being ready to use the deterrent within the narrowest feasible limits, as indispensable to making deterrence work. We reject the policy of national bluff which permits possession but does not permit its essential secondary intention. We discern no other way to defend the Constitution of the United States, to protect its institutions of liberty, and to prevent the most awful aggression against innocent peoples here and elsewhere. It would hardly be better for us if some other people bore this burden, but in any case there is none who can lift it from us. In due course, the Soviet Union may learn to prefer ways of peace abroad and ways of liberty at home—in which case, peace among nations may be possible. For this we labor and pray.

Conventional War and Nuclear War

Even should the specter of nuclear war be lifted at last from the human race, we recognize the horrors of modern conventional warfare. The power and terrible accuracy of rocket-driven conventional arms, launched at great distances, became visible during the last days of World War II. These horrors have been magnified since, as exhibited in the Falkland Islands and elsewhere. In World War I, 15 million civilians died. In World War II, 51 million civilians died. In some sixty-seven conventional wars since that time, millions of other civilians have died. It cannot be thought that an end to nuclear deterrence will necessarily usher in an era without war. Insofar as war springs from evil in the human heart, insofar as that evil is ineradicable except by the grace of God, and insofar as human beings can, and do, resist God's grace, we do not expect that war will ever be wholly eliminated from human history. Nonetheless, the dream of a world without war abides. Institutions of liberties and rights, peaceful competition and coopera-

67

tive labors, and the conversion of every human heart are devoutly to be labored for. They cannot be said to have yet been attained. Like Christ, we see ahead the cross: Not our will, but Thine be done.

Distinguished strategists have argued that an end to nuclear deterrence raises the probabilities of conventional war on the part of the Soviet Union. This is because of the great superiority of Soviet conventional forces, wherever they should choose to mass them, on the Central German Plain or on the northern borders of the Middle East.[29] However this may be, we hold it to be a good worth sacrificing for to raise the capabilities of NATO forces in Europe and the Middle East to a level sufficient to deter any Soviet temptation to aggression. The editors of *The Economist* have worked out a study of the as-yet unmet requirements of such sufficiency. They hold that this goal is costly, but attainable.[30] Economically, at least, it is feasible; whether political will for the sacrifices entailed is available is questionable. Still, the present weakness of NATO on the German plain now makes recurrence to defense with tactical nuclear weapons a necessary part of NATO strategy. To supplant this reliance on tactical nuclear weapons with a sufficient conventional deterrent seems to us both morally good and morally required. Even so, prudence requires that the nuclear deterrent must be held in reserve. Certainly, it will have to be so until the current imbalance in conventional forces is redressed. We urge speedy and generous cooperation to this end, even though welfare states naturally prefer to evade heavier expenditures except for social programs.

It has not been sufficiently recognized, in the U.S. and in Europe, that the people of the United States have made themselves hostage to an outbreak of war in Europe. Should such a war arise, and should a terrified Europe demand that tactical nuclear weapons be called into play (when, for example, Soviet troops had made a breakthrough across half of Germany), further nuclear escalation could not be ruled out, in which the Soviets would threaten the United States with nuclear destruction. To protect themselves from this possibility, the people of the United States might someday seek disengagement from the European theater. But this step, too, would have fateful consequences not only for Europe and the United States but for humankind. In this context, the cry for "no first use" of tactical or other nuclear weapons has for some much appeal. Heeding such a cry, the United States might at first save itself. It is not likely to have done so for long. Until an adequate conventional deterrent is in place in Europe, we hold a pledge of "no first use" to be divisive and destabilizing. Perhaps most clearly among our differences, this conviction differentiates our judgment from that of the bishops' second draft. Since NATO forces are not designed for offensive use, the question arises only in the case of Soviet aggression. Deterrence of that aggression is the first moral imperative. When NATO conventional forces are able to present a sufficient deterrent without recourse to nuclear weapons, such a pledge would be in effect whether stated or not.

Facing the Future

We do not consider the present situation of nuclear deterrence ideal; we consider it a moral choice involving the lesser evil. When we look to the future, we see both creative possibilities and even greater dangers. The greatest danger is spiritual. Democratic peoples find protracted danger and sacrifice more onerous by far than do the leaders of totalitarian states. The latter benefit by military mobilization; the former find it a threat to democracy itself. Again, successful deterrence buries the evidence that brought it into play to begin with, and a free people must take up the argument ever anew. Thus, hope for peace nourishes illusions in a democratic people, eternal vigilance being the price of liberty most difficult to pay. That is why today broad popular discussion, argument and consensus are indispensable to the preservation of liberty. The military strategy of the United States and its allies depends upon popular understanding and popular support.

In this respect, every citizen might well wish that our lives were not burdened, as they are, by sacrifices for defense. Many cannot help wishing that nuclear dangers might simply vanish. Indeed, much time and energy is well spent trying to imagine prudent steps to diminish the present danger.

Many citizens have hoped that a mutually verifiable nuclear freeze by both the U.S. and the USSR would offer surcease. We judge that the hope that the Soviets will consent to on-site verification is remote. We recognize that verification by technical means such as satellite observation and electronic monitoring is subject to deception and disinformation. Moreover, there are four reasons for believing that a freeze now would be destabilizing. First, the Soviet nuclear force already holds two destabilizing advantages, both in its first-strike capacity concerning the U.S. land-based

Minutemen and in its targeting of European capitals with SS-20s. Similarly, the trend lines of new Soviet developments are up, whereas the process of strengthening U.S. and NATO deterrent forces is appropriately democratic and slow. Second, a freeze at present levels does not at all diminish the present danger; it freezes it in place. This danger includes the rapidly approaching obsolescence of U.S. delivery systems and the relative youth of Soviet systems. Third, we note that a "verifiable" freeze—including a freeze upon nuclear research and development (which can go on inside buildings anywhere)—would require a massive regimen of verification beyond anything remotely sustainable at present. Finally, Soviet officials have begun offering schemes of reduction, below levels envisaged by a mere freeze. For these reasons, we judge that a negotiated freeze may well be inferior to negotiated reductions, and thus cannot be insisted on by moralists. Such concrete judgments must finally be resolved democratically, by duly constituted governments amid reasoned public debate, in which good people disagree.

Since the Soviets have several forms of superiority at present—not necessarily in every respect, but in some important ones—it is obviously difficult for Soviet leaders to surrender advantages they have amassed through great sacrifices on the part of their peoples. On the other hand, Soviet leaders have reason to fear the greater inventiveness of free societies. If American and NATO resolve were now to falter, Soviet leaders would have reason to continue their present successful strategy. If, on the contrary, they must face the fact that the U.S. is determined to maintain deterrence through new inventions, they may conclude that they must alter their course. The linchpin of preventing war is Soviet will. Soviet intentions, strategies, weapons development and procurement follow from Soviet will. At the present moment, we judge that negotiations for reductions in both strategic and theater nuclear weapons coincide with real interests on both sides. Such negotiations, however fragile and risky, as history shows, have a reasonable prospect of success, provided that the Soviets perceive greater risks in the determination of Western nations to rectify the current imbalance. Such an opportunity must be pursued, despite the sorry record of arms negotiations in the past. Caution is required since negotiations for the sake of negotiations may occasion greater evils. Criteria distinguishing moral from less than moral negotiations are required. Many of our current difficulties arise out of judgments made by American negotiators in the past. The current emphasis on large offensive land-based missiles, for example, and on offensive rather than defensive weapons, arose from past negotiations.[31] Nonetheless, a change in Soviet will, through negotiations if possible, is to be pursued with determination.

The question of defensive weapons raises further technological possibilities in the future. It is not our role to recommend particular weapons systems, but it is important to recall that technology does not stand still and that the future is not determined. Future developments in satellite detection systems, matched with nonnuclear satellite weapons, could enable defenders to destroy ballistic weapons shortly after take-off. Long-range ballistic missiles would, therefore, be rendered obsolete. Some experts hold that current technology affords just such a defensive possibility now, others believe this will not be feasible until well into the future, when laser weapons are available. In any case, this is a nonnuclear defense. As a deterrent system, it does not rely on counterforce or countervalue but on nonnuclear defensive instruments. Not only does its moral character seem to be superior, but its implementation would seem to remove the threat of land-based missile systems. While it is not our role here to pass judgment for or against this or other particular systems, we do wish to note that the present situation may one day be lifted from the human race. The human race is neither static nor foredoomed.

For most of its history, the human race did not live under nuclear threat; there is nothing inevitable or necessary about the continuance of that threat. Efforts to remove it must be sound, prudent, and wise, lest they result in a deterioration of the present situation into something even worse. But eventually to lift such a threat is surely within the reach of sustained moral efforts. It is the vocation of Christians and Jews not only to reflect on the world but to change it, bringing it closer to the outlines of the Kingdom promised in both the Old and the New Testaments. It is the vocation of American citizens, civilian and military, called by the Seal of the United States to evoke *Novus Ordo Seclorum*, a new order of liberty and justice for all, to extend the boundaries of liberty and justice by peaceful means, through the consent of the governed. Although not without failures and flaws, the purpose of United States foreign and military policy since World War II has been to defend and to extend such liberties, on which alone true peace can rest. We cherish the hope that even our adversaries will one day experience liberty for all their peoples, and join with us in the cooperative task of bringing all peoples on earth to a fuller measure of human development, in peace, liberty, and justice for all humankind, fulfilling thereby the will of God on earth. It is in seeking to follow His Will that we have, to the best of our ability, formulated these arguments for the respectful consideration of our fellow Catholics, our fellow citizens, and all persons of good will throughout the world. May God favor this purpose. Though His ways be dark, His constancy abides forever.

Co-Signers of "Moral Clarity in the Nuclear Age"

John Agresto
Richard Allen
Edward C. Arenz
Walter Baran
Catherine V. Barr
Jeffrey Bell
William J. Bennett
William H. Brady, Jr.
James W. Brennan, M.D.
John H. Bruce
Walter C. Bruschi, M.D.
Patricia A. Bryce
Patrick J. Buchanan
James L. Buckley
John J. Buckley
Robert J. Buckley
William F. Buckley, Jr.
Clarence Burley
James Carberry
James D. Carnes
Karen Carnes

William Carney (R-N.Y.)
Gertrude E. Connor
Brian J. Corcoran
Tom Corcoran (R-Ill.)
Robert Cynkar
Madeleine De Respinis
Patrick J. Donohoe
Jude P. Dougherty
Thomas R. Dye
John Erlenborn (R-Ill.)
Edward J. Feulner, Jr.
Donna R. Fitzpatrick
Vincent Fitzpatrick
Peter Flanigan
Luz G. Gabriel
Paul C. Goelz, S.M.
Peter Grace
Daniel O. Graham
Gustav Gumpert
Rev. Henry Haacke
Terry Hall

Elyse Harney
Bruno Heck
Edward L. Henry
John Hiler (R-Ind.)
John P. Hittinger
Russell Hittinger
Henry J. Hyde (R-Ill.)
Robert C. Jeffrey
Michael Joyce
Daniel Kelly
Martin J. Kilcoyne
Stephen A. Koczak
Adrienne M. Kosciusko
Alden J. Laborde
Richard A. Lamanna
Thomas Langan
Philip F. Lawler
Edward Littlejohn
Daniel J. Loden
Bill Lowery (R-Calif.)
Clare Boothe Luce
Richard B. Madden
Daniel J. Mahoney
Christopher Manion
Herbert J. Mellan
Mark Michalski
James Miclot
Ron Miele
Guy V. Molinari (R-N.Y.)
Donald J. Morrissey
Matthew Murphy
James P. McFadden

William McGurn
Ralph McInerny
Barbara Nauer
Michael Novak
James J. O'Rourke
Howard Penniman
Dino J. Pionzio
Thomas J. Powers, S.J.
John Putka, S.M.
Quentin L. Quade
Henry Regnery
Naomi Reiter
Charles W. Ross, Jr., O.S.J.
Bro. Owen Sadlier, O.S.F.
James V. Schall, S.J.
John Seiler
William E. Simon
Joe Skeen (R-N. Mex.)
Thomas Skladony
Robert L. Spaeth
William Stanmeyer
Edward Styles
Roseanne Talbot
Cecilia S. Thomas
William S. Thomas
Eugene S. Tighe, Jr.
Richard F. Timone, S.J.
Mrs. Emil C. Toedtli
Stephen Tonsor
Rev. Paul Trinchard
Charles L. Vaughan
William C. Vinet, Jr.

Scott Walter
Mark Weber
Vin Weber (R-Minn.)

John Hazard Wildman
Ellen Wilson
Phyllis Zagano

PART 2

Blessed be the LORD, my rock,
   who trains my hands for war,
and my fingers for battle;
   my rock and my fortress,
my stronghold and my deliverer,
   my shield and he in whom I take refuge,
who subdues the peoples under him.
                                    —Psalm 144

INTRODUCTION

On January 6, 1983, a first draft of "Moral Clarity" was sent to the Vatican for use in consultations by the Vatican Secretary of State. On January 17–19, I took part in a conference at the Konrad Adenauer Stiftung in Bonn, West Germany, and shared a copy with colleagues there, who received it enthusiastically. Later, in June, I was asked to deliver a paper in Bonn, looking at the moral question from the European standpoint.

Before and after the June conference, I drove through several of the classic centers of German Christian life. I visited the first Benedictine monastery established on German soil, in A.D. 746, at Ottobeuren; Trier, celebrating its 1999th year, the city of St. Ambrose, St. Augustine, St. Helena, and St. Athanasius; Maria Laach and Bonn; Heidelberg; Stuttgart (where I met the editors of the major Protestant journal, Evangelische Kommentare); and Munich. The gold and green fields of the rolling German countryside were in full early summer bloom, and village after village, their church spires seeking the sun, gleamed on the hillsides.

Yet Germany is today a land of tension. While I was in Bonn, masked rioters stoned the automobile of U.S.

Vice President George Bush in Krefeld, on the occasion of the 300th anniversary of the first German immigrants to the United States. Later, I met with panels of peace activists. Virtually all condemned the violence of "the few," described by some as "paid outsiders from West Berlin and Hamburg" and by others as "professional agitators, giving a bad name to the peace movement."

The world geopolitical situation looks different from Germany, the nation most on the front line of resistance. To a visitor from the continental United States, distances between cities seem small. One's eyes follow the trail of the swift-moving armies of 1940 and 1945. The scream of a military jet overhead places the plane many miles away. For jets, national borders are minutes apart.

So it is useful to seek moral clarity in a nuclear age from the perspective of European soil. The first of the three chapters which follow attempts to do this. The second considers the changes made by the U.S. Catholic bishops between autumn 1982 and May 1983 in subsequent drafts of their pastoral letter; from such advances, much is to be learned by all who walk the same terrain. The final chapter considers the question of just—and unjust—negotiations.

Chapter 2

THE GEOPOLITICAL SITUATION: A VIEW FROM EUROPE

At one time there was no comparison between the strength of the USSR and yours. Then it became equal. . . . Perhaps today it is just greater than equal, but soon it will be two to one. Then three to one. Finally it will be five to one. . . . With such nuclear superiority it will be possible to block the use of your weapons, and on some unlucky morning they will declare: "Attention. We're sending our troops into Europe, and if you make a move, we will annihilate you." And this ratio of three to one, or five to one, will have its effect: you will not make a move.

—Alexander Solzhenitsyn[1]

During the last ten years, there has been a great change in Western public opinion concerning nuclear weapons—and also a great change in reality. The change in reality is fundamental. At the time of the first SALT agreements in 1972, it was agreed that the Soviet Union through prodigious efforts since the Cuban missile crisis of 1962 had achieved "essential parity" with the U.S. From 1972 to 1980, three fundamental changes occurred: (1) The Soviet strategic nuclear forces grew at rates unmatched by the

United States; (2) Soviet *conventional* arms achieved virtual parity in quality with NATO conventional arms, while maintaining huge advantages in quantity; and (3) in 1979, the Soviets began placing European cities within the targeting mechanisms of a ring of powerful new SS-20s, against which the West had no appropriate dissuasion.

These fundamental changes in the balance of power in Europe—strategic nuclear, conventional, and theater nuclear—induce considerable fear. What is done with that fear is one of the great moral questions of our time.

This fear is entirely appropriate, because the nuclear initiative has, for the time being, passed to the Soviets. They have acted first and successfully. More profoundly, they now have a wider range of nuclear choices—and less constraint of every sort upon those choices—than NATO does. Andrei Sakharov addresses this point with some alarm:

> Precisely because an all-out nuclear war means collective suicide, we can imagine that a potential aggressor might count on a lack of resolve on the part of the country under attack to take the step leading to that suicide, i.e., it could count on its victim capitulating for the sake of saving what could be saved. Given that, if the aggressor has a military advantage in some of the variants of conventional warfare or—which is also possible *in principle*—in some of the variants of partial (limited) nuclear war, he would attempt to use the fear of further escalation to force the enemy to fight the war on his (the aggressor's) own terms. . . . Now take the next logical step—while nuclear weapons exist it is also necessary to have strategic parity in relation to

84

those variants of limited or regional nuclear warfare which a potential enemy could impose, i.e., it is really *necessary* to examine in detail the various scenarios for both conventional and nuclear war and to analyze the various contingencies. It is of course not possible to analyze fully all these possibilities or to ensure security entirely. But I am attempting to warn of the opposite extreme—"closing one's eyes" and relying on one's potential enemy to be perfectly sensible.[2]

My colleague, Irving Kristol, the distinguished editor of *The Public Interest*, holds that the nuclear umbrella which once protected Europe has now collapsed. It is no longer credible that United States' strategic nuclear weapons can deter an attack by Soviet conventional forces upon Europe, nor that they can deter a nuclear attack by the Soviets on some part of Europe. For why would the United States commit nuclear suicide? He argues, further, that the remaining 300,000 U.S. soldiers stationed in Europe no longer serve a useful purpose. On the contrary, he asserts, they expose the United States to nuclear blackmail, as hostages, and prevent the Europeans from becoming realistic about their own defense. He believes that reality will soon oblige the United States to withdraw its forces from Europe.

This view is extreme. But its logic, however much cold fear it induces, must be fully felt.

In a word, the Soviet SS-20s have already become one of the most successful weapons systems in the history of Europe; without ever being fired, they have shaken the ground. A kind of terror is in the air.

A first moral obligation is to still fear with the cool light of reason. Reason should never yield to terror.

Moreover, the lessons of 1938 are clear. Appeasement does not avert war; sometimes it makes war inevitable and more terrible than if determined resistance had been shown at earlier stages.

Much has been written about differences in perception concerning the Soviet Union. In recent debates, four different perceptions among Western Europeans have been recorded. (1) The Soviet Union and the United States are relatively *equal* threats to European safety and security; they are, in some ways, mirror images. European neutralism is the way to peace. (2) The Soviet Union is not so much an aggressive, expansionary power as a victim of historical paranoia, in part justified by current feelings of being surrounded by Western powers. (3) Correspondingly, leaders in the United States, particularly in the Reagan administration, overestimate "the Soviet threat," and lack the more balanced, nuanced view of Europeans who live closer to the USSR. (4) Most Europeans share a realistic view of Soviet power, roughly like that of the Americans, but differences of judgment about appropriate responses are many, both in Europe and in America.

Without getting into a debate about the nature and destiny of Soviet power, permit me only to make a crucial distinction between *intentions, proclivities,* and *strategic potential.* It seems to be a wise principle in charting any program of defense—whether in chess, in soccer, in commerce, or in military strategic thinking—to keep in mind a "worst case" view of the array of possibilities open to the opponent. A failure to do so invites terrible surprises, encourages complacency, and nourishes illusions.

First, one needs a clearheaded analysis of the range of options open to the strategic assets of the opponent. These represent the opponent's *strategic potential*. The factors involved include not only the technical capacities of its assets, but also its command and control capacities and its strategic doctrines. It is important to emphasize that strategic potential consists of more than material assets.

Second, one needs to analyze carefully the *proclivities* of an opponent. Of these the relevant components are, in one sense, more elusive and yet in another sense far better known. For these include factors of (a) history and culture, (b) institutions and the character of leadership, and (c) habits of mind and thought, including formal ideology and well-established patterns and habits of behavior. It was in some such sense, for example, that the American Founding Father James Madison said that the Constitution of the United States has its real existence, not in the "parchment barrier" of a few words on paper, but in the character and the institutions of the American people. In analyzing the proclivities of the Soviet Union, clear thought requires attention to the continuing power of Russian culture, to the tradition of old-fashioned Russian geopolitical ambition, to the actual weight of the Marxist-Leninist sense of historical destiny, and to the bureaucratic imperatives of the Soviet ruling elite. From such factors flow the spiritual component, the will, which actualizes strategic potential.

Third, one needs to estimate (since certain knowledge is not possible) the *intentions* of current leadership. Much more attention is usually given to intentions than to proclivities. This seems to be a mistake, because a grasp of intentions is inherently based upon a high degree of guesswork, whereas proclivities are far more stable, more knowable, and more closely related to real interests. In addition, the Leninist doctrine of the "correlation of forces" instructs Soviet leaders clearly enough to keep cool judgment about the probabilities of success and failure. Such judgment tilts Soviet analysis away from evanescent intentions and toward more secure and established proclivities. To be sure, totalitarian leadership is inherently vulnerable to naked seizures of will—*la feroce volontà* as Mussolini called it, and as Stalin exercised it. But "collective leadership" of the Soviet style and Marxist-Leninist doctrine mitigates this tendency.

All three factors are important. Moral analysis suggests that strategic potential and proclivities are the most decisive.

I raise these points at the beginning because the very first requirement of "just-war" thinking requires an exact analysis of "the just cause." If the Soviet Union were constituted as a nation like other nations, our task today would be far simpler than it is. When we in the West speak of "deterrence," we have in mind almost exclusively the deterrence of the Soviet Union. Our own democracies do not threaten one another. This is not only because we together form an alliance but, rather, because we each value self-determination, mutual collaboration in the pursuit of peaceful commerce and cultural interchange, and the beneficent (although difficult) rule of liberty and law. All our concentrated energy of deterrence crystallizes around one threat: that of the Soviet Union.

Here, indeed, Europeans may be by habit better analysts of the Soviet Union than we—so far away—in the United States. On the other hand, Europeans, especially younger Europeans, face special spiritual temptations which may blunt inherent European advantages. Having experienced two world wars on European soil in almost successive generations in this century, a third European war must seem, in a poignant way, unthinkable. Furthermore, from 1945 until the present—for almost forty years—a broken, and then a prosperous, Europe has counted on the United States' nuclear umbrella to keep war away. There must be immense disappointment in Europe, however irrational such a feeling might seem in the court of cold reason, that that nuclear umbrella has been pierced—as if the Americans should somehow have prevented it. There seems to be considerable anger at Americans among at least some small (but visible) parts of the population, and this anger seems coincident with the emergence of the three new strategic realities I mentioned at the outset: the tangible growth of the Soviet strategic nuclear, conventional, and theater nuclear power during the last four years.

It is neither just nor useful to blame Europeans for the sudden emergence of fear and misdirected anger, the underlying cause of which is actually a moral crisis. For societies which are simultaneously democratic, capitalist (or social market), and pluralistic carry within them two virtues which are also defects. First, productive of unprecedented prosperity and liberty (and which generation of European youths ever lived in greater personal abundance and liberty?), such societies soon erode the martial virtues. Based upon relations which are pacific, law-abiding, commercial, and libertarian, such societies almost by deliberation (certainly in the forethought of such architects of our present as Adam Smith and Montesquieu) discourage the taste for physical bravado, for martial glory, and even for the heroic, instilling instead a due regard for small gains and losses, for prudence and mutual regard, for practical accomplishment, and for a spirit of mutual adjustment and compromise. This is not the stuff of heroism, unless peace itself is an unheroic sort of life, given to smoothing troubled waters and concentrating attention on the calm resolution, rather than on the dramatic escalation, of passionate conflict. In short, the democratic, commercial, pluralistic spirit is quite different from the spirit of the knights and the feudal warlords, and the martial talents which distinguished the leadership of European civilization only a few generations ago.

> The old order was preoccupied with intangible goods to an extent we now hardly ever see. The king had his glory, the nobles their honor, the Christians their salvation, the citizens of pagan antiquity their ambition to outdo others in serving the public good. . . . The weightier truth, however, was that concern with these fancies skewed public policy and public budgets, sacrificing the real needs of the people to the petty desires of their governors.[3]

It is not easy to arouse democratic peoples to thoughts of wars, crusades, and noble military causes. People in the mass (those we used to call the common people), expressing themselves through self-government, seldom share the extreme spirituality of the clergy, the aristocrat's natural longing for glory, or the military's proper longing to demonstrate courage and competence in combat.

The second part of the crisis of the spirit flows from the same source. In order to function effectively, a society which is democratic, commercial, and pluralistic must quite deliberately avoid intense *official* concentration upon moral, spiritual, and religious matters. Pluralism and liberty of conscience exact this price. For in the depths of the human spirit, each person has an autonomy and personal responsibility which no official power can either take away or fully express. Public authorities—those of the state, of the universities, of the media of communication, and others—are obliged to maintain an historically unprecedented taciturnity. In the religious states of the past, in homogeneous states, public figures not only voiced the profound communal convictions of all, they *represented* them in their persons. When Charlemagne knelt to be crowned by the pope—as Napoleon wished to be, not yet two centuries ago—all Europe, in a sense, knelt with him. Such homogeneity of spirit is no longer thought to be appropriate to a people free and pluralistic in spirit, not precisely because the state is secular but because the state is pluralistic. A sort of spiritual abnegation is required in public, a refusal to exercise an *imperium* over conscience. This is, I think, a noble self-abnegation. But it exacts high costs.

One of those costs is that public figures—and again I insist that journalists, artists, professors, and many others bear the same costs as those borne by public officials—no longer effectively speak, in the full sense, as moral, spiritual, or religious authorities for all. This fact means that modern societies like those which compose NATO may at first appear to be spiritually empty. One phrase some religious writers use for this phenomenon is "practical atheism" or "practical materialism"—that is, not atheism or materialism in *principle*, but silence or emptiness or (more exactly) spiritual chastity, exactly where in earlier eras, not so long ago, there was public satisfaction.

Is it any wonder, then, that the immature eye, looking over our public life, should declare that Western Europe and the United States seem to be as spiritually empty as Eastern Europe, though rather in practice than in principle? This way of thinking is immature and dangerous. But it is common enough.

These are the two chief reasons why Western nations seem, at first glance, to be losing the battle of the human spirit. It is not easy for Western men and women in public roles to voice their most profound human convictions, their moral principles, or the secrets of their spiritual lives. Simple due regard for the analogous but quite different spiritual autobiographies of their colleagues and fellow citizens prevents them from seeming to demand full consent for what they themselves deem most important in human life, the springs of their own spiritual journey. To infer from this decent silence, this profound regard for others, a "spiritual emptiness" is a great error. In public, there *is* a spiritual emptiness, but out of self-abnegation and a true regard for the proper liberties of the human soul of each. This *system* denies itself what earlier types of social systems did not deny themselves. This is not a fault, but a high and precious virtue. Yet it is also, in public affairs, a serious weakness.

For human beings are, above all, symbolic animals. They hunger for publicly, communally acclaimed values. One sees this vividly in the young. The virtues of societies which are democratic, capitalist, and pluralistic are not easily learned by the young. These are, after all, the virtues acquired through the lessons of experience: realism, moderation, prudence, and a spirit of compromise and "loyal opposition" (in which one agrees, in civility, to disagree and to abide by consensual methods). These might be said to be the virtues of middle age, chary of the romantic sense of the young and not yet accustomed to the detached wisdom of the aged. Literature speaks well of the young and of the old. Religion, too, finds more direct access to the young and to the old. Middle age, less sung in song, is the age of activism in political economy.

When we come, then, to articulate our middle-aged reasons for our highest ideals, and for their defense against hostile forces, we find ourselves acting against our accustomed grain. Bishops easily enough speak of moral principles and high visions, and for that we may be grateful. Yet the task of those whose vocation calls them to make political economies work, and in particular adequately to defend themselves, demands far greater uncertainties, awareness of improbable contingencies, and an instinct for the difficulties in the execution of any alternative whatever.

We all wish that the threats which now face our civilization did not exist. We wish we did not have to face them. As President Kennedy once said: "Life is unfair." And he also spoke, in his inaugural address, of our generation's "call to bear the burden of a long twilight struggle, year in and year out," and he continued: "In the long history of the world, only a few generations have been granted the role of defending freedom in its hour of maximum danger. I do not shrink from this responsibility—I welcome it. I do not believe that any of us would exchange places with any other generation."[4] So is our struggle, still today, for moral clarity in a nuclear age.

Our cause is just, for the existence of our liberties is at risk. The disguised threat is that of living under intimidation, obliged to do what we would not choose to do, by some degree living under a regime to which we do not give free assent.

For nuclear weapons have four functions. The first is to yield a sense of sovereignty and prestige. Thus France and Britain have borne heavy expense to maintain an independent deterrent force, and the USSR has reasons beyond those of defense for its efforts to rank as the greatest of the "superpowers." The second is for intimidation, since nuclear arsenals speak louder than words and evoke in less well-armed neighbors both awe and respect. The third is for deterrence; the "nuclear umbrella" of the United States was once judged to be the most moral, least burdensome, and most effective method of containing Soviet ambitions with respect to Europe and Japan. The fourth is the function most popularly recognized, that of an actual instrument of war. It is important to recognize that the first three functions, whatever their individual merits, do not require the explosive use of nuclear weapons. The most popularly recognized and justly feared function of nuclear weapons, the last, is but one of four actual functions.

We have seen that a chief moral imperative of our

age is to prevent both the unjust military use of nuclear weapons in actual war and the unjust use of such weapons for purposes of intimidation. We have also observed, with the Second Vatican Council of the Roman Catholic church, that the existence of new scientific weapons obliges moralists to think about war "in a way entirely new." In practice, not everything about the morality of nuclear weapons is "entirely new." But one thing that is new concerns the intention proper to deterrence.

Some moralists wish to wash their hands of moral responsibility by saying that it is permissible to *possess* nuclear weapons, but wrong in any way to *use* them or to *intend* to use them in military combat. This is casuistry of the worst sort, based on moral approval for the function of deterrence. But, it falls then into two fallacies. The first fallacy is that the mere possession of nuclear weapons will deter an aggressor, since the aggressor will not "believe" that the weapons will remain unused. The supposition that an aggressor will refrain from provocations, probes, and tests of will is an exceedingly dangerous one. The true intention of this so-called moral position is that of Pilate; to wish to pretend to moral responsibility by indulging in hypocrisy.

The second fallacy is to suppose that the *possession* of a nuclear deterrent does not itself include *intentions*. In a free society, citizens must vote the funds; parliamentarians must allocate them; military strategists must design the deterrent; companies must build its material components; officers and men must be trained to keep it in readiness A deterrent is not inert metal; it is an intentional process, which must be held always at the ready. Intentions are not solely internal subjective acts; they are also organizing principles of activity. The young enlisted man of eighteen who boards a Trident submarine as it leaves for its duty station is engaged in *intentional* activity, whatever his subjective state of mind.

Thus, it is simply not possible to possess a deterrent *without exercising its inherent intentionality.* The concept of a deterrent necessarily includes both an internal organizing principle (an intention in that sense) and an implied threat to the one who is being deterred (an intention in that further sense). The concept of a deterrent which has no intention and makes no threat is empty. No one could be led to such a concept except through moral evasion.

Next, we must note that the concept of intention must be applied differently in two different cases: (1) a direct premeditated, unconditioned action; (2) an action of deterrence. To intend to *do* something and to intend to *prevent* something are two different types of action. Furthermore, the act of deterrence typically embodies a threat, although of a peculiar sort. A parent often tells a child, "I'll tan your hide!" or voices a similar fearsome threat. Policemen carry threatening equipment. Embassies are guarded. Crowd control at a peaceful concert often involves mounted police or police with dogs. Deterrence is necessary in ordinary, peaceful human life because human behavior is not always rational. One would wish (even God would wish) that human beings loved God freely and willingly followed His law; just in case, the fires of Gehenna are invoked as a deterrent.

Indeed, the peace movement depends indispensably upon the deterrent value of images of mass destruction. Without this threat, the movement would lack passion.

The peculiar structure of intention in deterrence deserves clarification. It is true that if in premeditated resolution an assassin sets out to murder the pope, but fails, then he has "already committed murder in his heart," and *morally speaking* (even *legally speaking*) is as guilty in the attempt as in its success. But the case of those who intend to deter such an act is quite different. If one's premeditated resolution is to *deter* an assassin, then the intention is fulfilled if and only if the deterrence works—a potential assassin is kept out of reach, is discouraged, or is detected and disarmed. Should one actually have to *use* one's deterrent weapons, a *breakdown* in deterrence is deemed to have occurred. At this point, deterrence is no longer the operating activity from a moral point of view; one must shift to the logic of direct action.

With respect to the nuclear deterrent, its fundamental intention is to deter unjust aggressive actions by another. "To do good and to avoid evil" is the fundamental moral law, under which such a fundamental intention clearly falls. A complication arises because inherent in the organizing principle of deterrence is an intention of conditional use; an effective deterrent tells a potential aggressor: "Avoid evil acts lest you be punished by my deterrent force." The will to inflict punishment is inherent in the deterrent. Without such will, the "deterrent" becomes a symbol of law and reason only, perhaps like the ceremonial pikestaffs of the Swiss Guards in the Vatican. Ceremonial deterrents are not designed to deter a determined aggressor, only one already committed to justice and to law.

At this point, some question the moral validity of the nuclear deterrent, not insofar as it is a deterrent, but insofar as it requires a will to punish the aggressor in case deterrence fails. This formulation, however, shows that their moral objection does not aim directly at deterrence, whose moral legitimacy it concedes. It aims, rather, at the *breakdown* of deterrence. Yet if we ask what might cause deterrence to break down or, conversely, how we might best contrive to make certain that it does *not* break down, we see immediately that the greatest moral danger lies in an inadequate deterrent. The logic of nuclear deterrence is to prevent certain forms of unjust aggression and, further, to prevent any use of nuclear weapons whatever. Only in the fulfillment of these two goals does deterrence fulfill its mission. This mission is moral. Indeed, the sacrifices and disciplines required to maintain its vigilance require high moral courage and nobility of soul.

Those responsible for the breakdown of deterrence, therefore, bear a tragic moral responsiblity. Even the attempt to acquire deterrence "on the cheap" seems, in this light, morally reprehensible. For doubts about the adequacy of deterrence positively solicit bold and aggressive probes. Doubts about Western resolve clearly underlie the bold Soviet program of building an "iron ring" of SS-20s just behind the Iron Curtain. Given Soviet *proclivities* to advance wherever weakness is apparent, the attempt by Western powers to buy deterrence "on the cheap" during the 1970s illustrates the moral peril into which illusions quickly plunge the morally weak.

A plausible rejoinder to this line of argument is that it seems to lead inexorably into "an arms race," with each side expending ever new resources to keep deterrence credible. Three points need to be observed. First, sheer material obsolescence requires fresh generational expenses simply to replace old equipment. (The generational retirement of obsolescent systems which have never been used in war is the clearest possible evidence that deterrence works.)

Second, despite popular perceptions to the contrary, spending on *conventional* arms is far more expensive, by a factor of at least nine to one, than spending on the nuclear deterrent. In the United States, military spending in constant 1983 dollars dropped 19 per cent between 1970 and 1981, from $223.1 to $181.5 billion. Throughout that period spending on nuclear weapons constituted only eight per cent of all military spending.[5]

Third, the generational replacement of the nuclear deterrent—a process which typically requires fifteen years—affords each new generation of leaders an opportunity to think anew about *moral improvements* in the nature of weapons systems.[6] In the first generation, for example, from about 1945 to 1960, the *moral character* of the deterrent force was at its crudest. During this period, the United States had a virtual nuclear monopoly. Its first generation of warheads was characterized by very large megatonnage and only marginal accuracy, so that their main threat was to Soviet urban centers. This system was the least moral.

The second generation of U.S. systems, put in place in the 1960s, was composed of much smaller warheads and more accurate guidance systems. As the Soviet systems grew in size, this period was at first characterized by the relatively simple but still crude design of Mutual Assured Destruction. Each side targeted the other's cities. But a more sophisticated and, from a moral point of view, much superior strategy of deterrence began to evolve: "Flexible Response." This strategy permitted the targeting of military targets in addition to, or rather than, urban populations.

Finally, in the third stage of development, beginning about 1975, advances in technology permitted the construction of smaller warheads with far greater accuracy. Clear advances were made in the direction of *proportionality* and *discrimination*. So great were these advances, indeed, that some moralists began to worry that nuclear strategy might be becoming too "reasonable," by beginning to fall into the classical moral logic that governs large conventional weapons. They began to fear that the smaller nuclear weapons were beginning to resemble (in proportionality and discrimination) the larger conventional weapons. They applauded this development for its superior moral structure, but they also began to fear that the psychological barrier between conventional warfare and nuclear warfare was beginning to weaken. Moreover, the continuing existence of large warheads and vastly increased throwweight (especially on the Soviet side) afforded an ominous backdrop to the newer, smaller, and more accurate weapons. Some moralists, therefore, fell into moral conflict in their own minds, torn between approval of weaponry more proportional and discriminating, on the one hand, and fears about lowering the threshold of horror which accrues to *all* nuclear weapons.[7]

During these last three systemic generations, deterrence has been based upon *offensive* weapons rather than upon *defensive* weapons. This fact presents a moral challenge for our own generation. The *moral superiority* of defensive weapons is obvious. For the right to self-defense—and for states, the *duty* of self-defense—is much more neatly underlined by defensive than by offensive deterrents. Furthermore, in the interests of mutual stability, nations intent solely upon self-defense may quite reasonably *share* the technology of defensive systems with their foes. President Reagan, accordingly, has made just this offer to the Soviets, looking ahead to the strategy of deterrence a generation from now. Secondly, a defensive shield is much more clearly a "nuclear umbrella" than is an offensive deterrent. It is intellectually conceivable—and perhaps technically feasible, a judgment not for the moralist but for scientists to assess—that current arsenals of Intercontinental Ballistic Missiles (ICBMs) might one day be rendered obsolete. For if it were possible accurately to detect and swiftly to destroy offensive weapons shortly after their blastoff, such weapons would become a threat not to their intended targets but to their resident possessors.

Admittedly, we now enter the realm of speculation about future possibilities. But this very fact is evidence of sound moral thinking. For moral thinking is, first of all, thinking about possible better futures, about ends and purposes, about creative advances. The human race is not condemned forever to immobility and resignation to the present. Human intellect and will are free.

Consider the alternatives advanced by rival futurists. Jonathan Schell in *The Fate of the Earth* imagines that the future solution to present dilemmas lies in a benign, tolerant, peaceful, rational "world government."[8] The Catholic bishops of the United States even propose the model of the United Nations as a harbinger of such a development![9] Yet the minute one tries to imagine the conversion of the Soviet Union to the ideals of such a vision of world government, one sees the absurdity of the wish. The solution proposed is merely a wishing away of the problem to be met. The sole problem arises from the nature of the Soviet Union. Against no other nation is nuclear deterrence necessary. Those who argue that the government of the United States is also a potential threat cannot, logically, have faith in the moral quality of *world* government, if civil democratic government cannot even guarantee moral confidence in the United States.

Still others, such as William Colby, react to present perplexities by urging a "freeze." Yet it is difficult to see how this is anything but a counsel of despair; a "freeze" does nothing to remove current inadequacies in deterrence. Quite the contrary. It locks in place exactly those sorts of imbalances which have generated the current wave of fear. Its true message is not, as it says, that the arms race is "blind" but that, just as blindly, human beings can do nothing but say "halt." Under the lash of fear, the freezing of the human capacity to think and to act is understandable, but it is hardly admirable and not in the least hopeful. Moreover, the hidden condition for a successful freeze lies in its demand upon the USSR to permit the on-site verification of nuclear weapons deployed (many of them undetectable by satellite technology) and of easily disguised research and development. This condition requires a hopefulness about Soviet proclivities which seems counterfactual to history. It must also be counted as a wishing away of the fundamental problem.

Finally, there are some—including certain passages in the U.S. bishops' pastoral letter—who are already imagining preemptive surrender. Contemplating Eastern Europe, some are already saying that they would willingly live under such a regime, addressing against it "civilian resistance" and "passive resistance," in the confident hope that after two or three generations they would "convert" it from within. Their confidence in their own virtue—which, of course, they attribute to their faith in God—is quite touching. Do they imagine themselves as future Orlovs, Sakharovs, and Solzhenitsyns? Since they are willing to renounce their moral obligation to defend the innocent from unjust aggression, one wonders what next moral renunciation they will make. Perhaps they think that "liberation theology" will enable them to subvert Marxism-Leninism through Christian Marxism. They do not seem to glimpse the contempt in which they will properly be held by their new masters, who will judge that their unwillingness to fight for the institutions of liberty constitutes a preemptive devaluation of such institutions. This devaluation is already quite congenial to those whom they aim to "convert."

All of these alternatives—world government, a freeze, and preemptive surrender—share a common theme. Each is naive about political institutions. Each has in mind the freedom of the moral individual, *as if this freedom were not constituted by specific institutions of*

103

civil and political liberties: parliaments, opposition parties, courts, a free press, private property, a limited state, and the like. Thus, "world government" implies that all the world shares the habits, values, and institutional forms of civil discourse and the consent of the governed. The freeze depends upon the Soviet Union becoming an open society.[10] Preemptive surrender rests upon a thoroughly spiritual and nonpolitical vision of Christianity and civilization. In short, in the name of "preserving the values of the West," each overlooks the *nature* of Western achievements. These achievements lie precisely in the development of specific kinds of political and economic *institutions,* built up through centuries of moral thinking, political struggle, and no little bloodshed. All this is now to be counted as nothing, in the light of "higher" spiritual values. In the place of humble, imperfect but manifestly functioning institutions, we are instructed to trust the spiritual life of individuals.

The West has already had many historical battles with the Gnostics, the Cathars, and spiritualists of every sort. What the West has learned from such struggles is the self-abnegation required to build humble institutions which promise utopias to none but liberty and due regard for individual rights to all. The "values" of the West most now to be defended are not so much "spiritual" as "political": incarnated in specific institutions. Those who love these institutions, and who intend to defend them with their lives, their fortunes, and their sacred honor, are *not* defending "spiritual values" in the abstract, but rather those *institutions* which permit individuals, alone or in association, to follow truth, conscience, and love wherever these may lead. Concrete institutions are the objects of our loyalty and our devotion. It is these which we defend against all enemies. It is around these institutions, through them, and by their empowerment of our diverse consciences that we intend to deter every threat from every enemy, in whatsoever form it may come.

In this respect, our purposeful public silence about the spiritual values that diversely move each of us is not a weakness. We love, and we will defend, the *institutions* which permit to us such respectful public silence, for only such institutions, bloody history has taught us, truly liberate the human soul.

Chapter 3

RESCUED FROM DISASTER: THE BISHOPS SPEAK OUT

Introduction

In an unprecedented way, the Presbyterians, evangelical churches, Methodists, and many other church leaders have begun to follow the lead of Roman Catholic bishops, who in 1982 and 1983 were featured often on cover stories of Time *and* Newsweek, *and extensively covered on television. Many various Christian bodies are now issuing statements on morality in a nuclear age, more or less drawing on the example—often the actual text—of the Catholic bishops.*

The process of preparing the U.S. Catholic pastoral letter was open, public, and two years in duration. Intense public debate, from citizens of all political and religious points of view, accompanied the process. Three different drafts were presented for public criticism, one in the late spring of 1982, one in the autumn, and a third on May 2–3, 1983, when 289 Catholic bishops assembled at the Palmer House in Chicago to amend and finally to approve the completed document.

The very fact that the moral and religious dimensions of nuclear defense are now being publicly discussed is a great advance for Christian sophistication. Yet such matters are controversial, and Christians of good will—united in baptism—retain their inherent duties of personal fidelity to reflective conscience. On such matters, Christians "agree to disagree," united in their mutual faith and love, while submitting all arguments to critical theological scrutiny. The issues are fateful for all of us. The broadest possible debate among citizens is profoundly desirable—conducted both in charity and with flinty intellectual integrity.

To their credit, the Catholic bishops of the United States prepared their newly approved pastoral letter, "The Challenge of Peace: God's Promise and Our Response," in an open and public fashion unprecedented in history. Long after the first two drafts appeared, in spring and autumn 1982, any Catholics or others who wished to have their views heard, privately or publicly, had the opportunity to join the argument. Compared to some of the extreme formulations of drafts one and two, the third draft, completed in late March and approved (with amendments) by a vote of 238 to 9 on May 3, 1983, represented an immense step forward. But getting there was crazy.

After a very long year's roller coaster of debate, during which the pacifist Left seemed to be mobilizing for an inquisition against the Reagan administration, events took a comical turn in late March, just after the third draft appeared. Pacifists in Chicago had been gathering 100,000 signatures in support of the bishops; traditionalists had been gathering counter-signatures. When they saw the third draft, the two groups almost changed sides.

Then, on May 2 and 3, the bishops assembled in the Windy City and, after a blizzard of contrary amendments, joyously delivered themselves of their long burden. Since then, practically everyone has declared that, while this or that passage displeases him, the document represents a victory for his point of view.

For this modern miracle, Joseph Cardinal Bernardin, Archbishop of Chicago and a prudent man, deserves a great deal of credit, along with Archbishop John R. Roach of St. Paul, current president of the Bishops Conference, who stood with him in the necessary balancing act. Cardinal Bernardin drove his five-bishop drafting committee to prior consensus on every line, and he managed an emotional two-day meeting in Chicago, which could easily have been stampeded, toward the best achievable outcome under the circumstances. Those circumstances included a two-year lobbying campaign in the public media by the formidable clerocracy of the Catholic Left.

Archbishop John R. Quinn of San Francisco, a former president of the conference and one of the more assertive of the bishops, moved certain last-minute changes that made the final document, by his lights, more "prophetic." *Time* reports his exultation: "We have done a great service to our country and to the world." That was, surely, the intention. History (and God Himself) will judge the actual result.

The Economist, before seeing the final text, was less sanguine than the good archbishop, noting the "philosophical tightrope-walking" of the bishops' reasoning on deterrence: "The bishops therefore allow the weapons but remove the moral justification for the only official use they have in the present debate, which is to deter the other side."

This is much too strong. The Catholic Left, institutionalized now as never before in a clerocracy (to distinguish organizational activists from ordinary pastors), is exultant because of one symbolic change made in Chicago. In their "support for immediate, bilateral, verifiable agreements to halt the testing, production, and deployment of nuclear-weapons systems," the bishops resoundingly changed the verb *curb* in the third draft back to the second draft's *halt*. A footnote now explains that this change does not place episcopal authority behind any particular political tactic, like the "freeze" resolution passed in the U.S. House of Representatives the very next day. Hairsplitters may argue that *halt* does, or does not, mean "freeze." Certainly, the bishops could have voted for "freeze"; a majority passionately so inclined seems to have been present. *Halt* was a compromise verb.

Mush or Meat?

Left-wing Catholics, represented by the *National Catholic Reporter,* were downcast by the third draft; one called it a bowl of "mush." Yet after an adroit use of the media in Chicago, the same Left wildly declared a victory. Since *halt* is a political judgment, not a theological one, however, the central enthusiasm of the Left stands clear. *Politically,* one can agree, red meat was thrown to the Left; the Reagan administration was publicly taunted. *Theologically,* the Left was soundly defeated. The proper province of bishops is theology.

This was the fundamental point made again and again in the approved letter: The authority of the bishops has full force on matters of faith and morals, but not on matters of prudential judgment. The latter includes both the interpretation of current events and concrete choices of tactics or strategy. If the bishops voted for *halt*, they did so precisely not as bishops but as U.S. citizens, with all the freedoms attached thereto. Considering the matter gravely, other U.S. citizens, including Catholics, are fully entitled to dissent.

The Vatican itself insisted upon this distinction in a critical memorandum recording the minutes of a meeting in Rome on January 18 and 19,[1] to which the U.S. principals were summoned to hear from certain concerned European prelates and the Vatican secretary of state. At this meeting, according to the published record, the Vatican discreetly voiced nine fundamental points, of which the most important was the one just mentioned:

> The [second] draft mixes different levels of authority and it will be difficult for the reader to make the necessary distinctions. Hence grave questions of conscience will arise for Catholics. A clear line must be drawn between the statement of principles and practical choices based on prudential judgment. When bishops offer elements for reflection or when they wish to stimulate debate—something that for pastoral reasons they might be called upon to do in present-day situations—they must do it in such a way that they clearly differentiate this from what they are bound to propose as *doctores fidei* [teachers of the faith]. . . .
>
> When differing choices are equally justifiable, bishops should not take sides. Rather they should offer several options or express themselves hypothetically.

The Vatican memo further asked that the pastoral letter "at least be rewritten to state clearly the different levels of authority," for several reasons:

> First, in respect for the freedom of the Christian so that he or she be clearly informed about what is binding in conscience. Second, in respect for the integrity of the Catholic faith so that nothing be proposed as doctrine of the Church that pertains to prudential judgment or alternative choices. Third, for reason of ecclesiology, that the teaching authority which belongs to each bishop not be wrongly applied and therefore obscure its credibility.

The Vatican had eight other points to make. Each is worth bearing in mind because each was heeded by the American bishops' third draft, often in the very same words.

2. *No first use.* The Vatican observed that the second draft had contained "an apodictic moral judgment rejecting first use of nuclear weapons, although the affirmation in the same text 'that serious debate is under way' does not seem to warrant such a statement, which remains highly contingent." The Vatican also saw the possibility of "first use as still necessary at this stage within the context of deterrence."

3. *Counterpopulation warfare.* "The draft pastoral letter should therefore state more clearly what is meant by condemnation of counterpopulation warfare, taking into account the contingency of judgment," the Vatican said, observing that throughout the Rome meeting questions were raised "about the application of the principle to actual nuclear strategies

or to the use of particular nuclear weapons. Such application entails a contingent judgment."

4. *Limited nuclear war.* "Although the meeting did not go into a detailed discussion of this point, it was thought that the text should clearly state to what extent the episcopal teaching authority can be committed when the draft itself states that 'technical opinion on this question and the writings of moralists remain divided' and when it recognizes 'that the policy debate on this question is inconclusive.'"

5. *The use of Scripture.* "It should also be made clear that [the second draft's] 'believing that peace is possible' expresses not a credal judgment but a mere conviction." The Vatican memo further attacked the second draft's assertion that "all of us have firm reasons for believing that God is truly bringing about his kingdom of justice and peace, and that we can look to a future in which all God's people, even those who may be considered 'enemies,' will live together in peace." Of this pap, the Vatican said succinctly: "Here again the text should clearly avoid mixing up two distinct levels and differing realities: our faith that the kingdom of God will come, and the realization that it is not certain if and when true peace will effectively exist in the world that is ours."

6. *The pacifist "tradition."* The Vatican memo "clearly affirmed that there is only one Catholic tradition: the just-war theory, but that this tradition was subject to inner tensions coming from an ever-present desire for peace. The relevant passage in the [second] draft letter would therefore have to be re-elaborated because it relates also to other affirmations that follow."

The memo tartly notes that the second draft "in

speaking about nonviolence and just war seems to propose a double Catholic tradition: a tradition of nonviolence and a tradition along the lines of the just-war theory that existed throughout the history of the Church." The memo cautions: "Other participants indicated that nonviolence has never been seen in the Church as an alternative to the just-war theory. The affirmation in the draft that 'the witnesses to non-violence and to Christian pacifism run from some Church fathers through Francis of Assisi to Dorothy Day and Martin Luther King' is factually incorrect." The Vatican memo questions whether there is a pacifist tradition holding "that any use of military force is incompatible with the Christian vocation." It doubts that in leading theologians in the first four centuries "there was a certain level of opposition to military service based upon particular Gospel passages." The pacifism of the second draft went too far for the Vatican.

7. *Deterrence.* "With regard to the morality of deterrence, several observations were made. Some participants suggested that this is one of the more difficult questions placed before the moral judgment of pastors and faithful. It must be seen in the wider context of the geopolitical situations and considerations. Its evaluation must take into account the existence of actual and probable threats of aggression. It cannot be separated from moral considerations and from prudential judgment on military and political facts and strategies. It has also a psychological component since it requires credibility to be effective."

8. *The* two *evils to be avoided.* Pope John Paul II's statement at the UN (June 11, 1982) justifying deter-

rence as an interim measure is, the memo observed, the bedrock of Catholic teaching. Cardinal Casaroli, Vatican secretary of state, on the basis of his knowledge of the pope's text and its context, noted in the memo *two* distinct dangers: "(a) the danger of *nuclear conflict*" and "(b) the endangering of *the independence and freedom of entire peoples.*" Casaroli elaborated:

> In both cases the concern is about vital values for peoples and for humanity. A question worthy of careful examination is whether there exists a relationship of equality or of superiority between the two above-mentioned points of consideration.
>
> There is a clear moral responsibility to do everything possible with total commitment and good will to prevent both the above dangers by the use of political means (negotiations, etc.). The Church has the responsibility to encourage, exhort, admonish, foster, and promote [these] with forcefulness and resoluteness, in season and out of season.
>
> While in active expectation that this goal might be obtained, and, in the opinion of many, in order to achieve this, there is what can be called a common conviction (in the West, but also in the East) that the only practical means at our disposal to avoid the *two* dangers—and which in substance at least has proven to be effective—is for the time being a sufficient *deterrence* (i.e., in fact, today, a nuclear deterrence). This is so despite the sum total of problems and risks that everyone, it can be said, recognizes in this means: the cost; a climate of suspicion and mistrust; the danger that with the existence of such weapons one might make use of them either willfully or even in ways that are not completely premeditated; etc.

9. The whole of Cardinal Casaroli's remarks deserve close study; the ninth especially deserves to be kept in mind:

> One must not give the impression that the Church does not take sufficiently into account the magnitude of the problems and the seriousness of the tremendous responsibilities of government authorities who have to make decisions in these matters. This does not mean that the Church cannot and must not clearly enunciate the certain and seriously obligatory moral principles that the authorities themselves must keep in mind and follow. This must be done, however, in such a manner that it helps those authorities to get a correct orientation according to the basic principles of human and Christian morals and not to create even greater difficulties for them in an area so enormously difficult and so full of responsibility. The same observations apply also to public opinion.

One closes this document from the Vatican with the sense that it is far wiser, infinitely more realistic, and much more sophisticated than the itchings and urgings of the most extremist American bishops— Gumbleton, Quinn, Hunthausen, Matthiesen, Sullivan, Kenny, and others—longing for confrontation with their government at any cost. Such bishops speak often of "prophecy," but fail to note that most prophets are false prophets. Further, as Eric Voegelin has pointed out, the greatest itch of our own day, masked by utopian and prophetic claims about a blissful future, is a self-destructive Gnosticism, a parody of true faith. The Vatican has diagnosed this malady in the earlier drafts exactly.

As it happens, the eight points made by the Vatican were those also at the top of the lists of many American Catholics, once they had seen the first draft last spring. For example, *Commonweal* (May 6) supported four of these points, as they became clear in the third draft; this should not have been a surprise, since the points are either classical, or matters of simple realism:

1. The third draft now makes crystal clear Rome's classic distinction between the bishops' authority on matters of universal moral principles and on matters of prudential judgment. Without this, the bishops would have been guilty of clerical hubris, invading the sphere of lay conscience and responsibility.

2. The section on deterrence now rests its center of gravity on the classic statement by Pope John Paul II on the justice of deterrence as an interim measure, and avoids several of the faults of earlier drafts.

3. The third draft takes into account both practical realities and the legitimate fears of European bishops concerning the premature declaration of "no first use" before a conventional deterrent is in place. By amendment, the U.S. bishops still want "no first use," as, in principle, everybody does. But interim deterrence is still the reality.

4. A more "unvarnished view of Soviet brutality and domination" (as *Commonweal* puts it) is in the final text, at one point relying heavily on a long passage from Pope John Paul II. This realistic view of the Soviets is the sole "just cause" for deterrence, the very first condition in just-war theory. Logically, this

passage belongs at the top of the section on deterrence.

In addition, my own list included:

5. The rather scandalously weak section in the first two drafts, confusing Holy Scripture with utopian worldly hopes. This has been completely rewritten for the third draft. While the final draft is still not as good as it could be, the scandal is diminished. For the Scriptures are written for human beings in every condition, whether in peace or in war, whether imprisoned or free, whether in despair or in hope. The peace of God is *not* the peace of this world. God's promises are not completely fulfilled in this life.

Faith, Work, and Fighting

In this respect, the second part of the title of the pastoral, "God's Promise and Our Response," does not yet seem quite right. God does *not* promise us the peace of this world; justice does *not* always permit us to seek only peaceful means, although always so until last, reluctant, limited resort. The final draft splendidly cites Pius XII on this point. Further, seeing what God asked of His Son (and the long suffering of His chosen people), *we* can hardly expect utopia for ourselves. John Paul II is cited here. Without a willingness to do battle for justice down through the centuries, our current liberty freely to seek God would not have been won. As Reinhold Niebuhr wrote in launching *Christianity and Crisis* early in 1941, during another high tide of pacifism in the churches:

Our civilization was built by faith and prayers and hard work—it was also built by fighting. Is there a Christian minister who believes that the rights which he daily enjoys and which he takes for granted, like the air he breathes, would be his to enjoy unless these rights had been fought for by Cromwell, by William of Orange, and by Washington? Are Protestants in the United States to live off the liberties which others are maintaining for them and then express complete indifference to the fate of those whose sacrifice makes the tranquil and serene life of American Christians possible? Should this become the American Protestant attitude toward the world, it would inscribe one of the darkest pages in the annals of the Church.

6. The first and second drafts violated the first principle stated in the Vatican memo, the distinction between universal moral principles and concrete prudential judgments, in aligning episcopal authority improperly behind too many *specifics* about particular weapons systems and particular forms of negotiations toward disarmament. The third draft—except for the emotional, symbolic need to say *halt* rather than *curb*— is far more chaste and principled. Specifics, even including some statements by current administration officials, have now been quite properly relegated to footnotes.

7. A sharp distinction is drawn, as the Vatican suggested, between pacifism as a personal option and pacifism as public policy. For nineteen hundred years—and in the practice of Jesus Himself—Catholic thinkers have rejected pacifism as the main teaching of the Catholic church. In public policy, any polity is bound by duties of self-defense. Pacifism is com-

manded neither in public policy nor, in fact, in personal life. On these matters, there is only one main tradition in the church, as the Vatican made clear, the just-war tradition. For the clergy, pacifism is a special symbolic vocation, suggesting transcendence and the better realities of the eschaton. At best, pacifism is an option for certain special consciences. On these matters, the final text is grudgingly clear enough. Its fundamental fault is not to have listed all the classical reasons why Christians have perennially rejected pacifism. These reasons are scriptural, theological, historical, political, and moral; they deserve to have been marshaled in this letter. It is honorable to permit pacifism; it is less so to fail to criticize it.

These were the seven major objections many of us had on matters of principle, and the final draft respects all seven, as the first two drafts did not. How can we not be exhilarated by this happy fruit of "an open church"? Cardinal Bernardin said that the bishops listened to their domestic critics, but it no doubt mattered more that the Vatican spoke.

The Chicago meeting opened with Cardinal Bernardin carefully explaining the eight points made by the Vatican, now fixed firmly in the text. Just how effective the Vatican—or simple good sense—was may be gleaned from the turning point of the Chicago meeting. After the first afternoon's vote on *halt* and a string of minor verbal successes, pacifist bishops crowded around the press tables making sure the press knew they were suddenly gaining "more ground than we hoped." Then, on the second day, Archbishop Quinn moved that the third draft's "*profound skepticism* about the moral acceptability of any use of nuclear weapons" be replaced. He was far more apodictic, proposing "*opposition on moral grounds* to any use of nuclear weapons." Drifting in that direction, the bishops voted approval. Then Cardinal Bernardin took the microphone and said in so many words: "The drafting committee considered that issue very carefully and, *given our discussions in Rome,* it decided against." A stir, another motion, and the bishops reversed themselves. From then on, many such amendments failed, illuminating the exact limits of the text.

A typical failure, expressing the underlying direction of the first and second drafts, was moved by Archbishop Hunthausen of Seattle: ". . . any attempt to seek superiority in nuclear weapons, or to develop weapons with first-strike capability, or even which can be reasonably construed as having first-strike capability, violates our conditional acceptance of the morality of deterrence. Such actions, therefore, are to be condemned." Only a handful of bishops voted yes. The archbishop conceded later that the document does not advocate unilateral disarmament, as he had hoped. He looked toward a better future.

One more example shows just how far—but no further—the bishops were willing to stretch the Vatican's position. In an earlier draft, the bishops had encroached on the Vatican's devaluation of pacifism only a little: "When any issue of peace or war is addressed, the nonviolent tradition must be part of the discussion." (In a pluralist society and church, how could it not?) The amendment, which passed, puffed out pacifism somewhat further: "While the just-war theory has clearly been in possession for the last fifteen hundred years of Catholic thought [Jesus and the disciples speaking to the centurions are conveniently forgotten], the 'new moment' in which we find ourselves sees the just-war theory and nonviolence as distinct but interdependent methods of evaluating warfare. They diverge on some specific conclusions, but they share a common presumption against the use of force as a means of settling disputes." This is, of course, a self-serving amendment on the part of the pacifist bishops. Its glorification of the "new moment" as a warrant is positively Gnostic. One may imagine what some "new moment" will justify next—this new source of authority, given the weight of Scripture and tradition.

Most of the passion and emotion for the past year has centered on the second of the letter's four chapters, on deterrence. The part of chapter 1 dealing with scriptural foundations, as we have seen, has been thoroughly rewritten. Chapter 4, consisting largely of pious sentiments addressed to various categories of believers, is disappointing. (Worse, it again heaps praise on pacifists, indicating thereby who are the best-organized lobbyists in the current church, warning them not at all of the typical pacifist sins and blindnesses, and flattering them—or, in the case of pacifist bishops, flattering themselves.)

Chapter 3, "The Promotion of Peace," is intended to be the positive centerpiece of the document. Much of it is new in the third draft. Thus, its proposals for a national peace academy and for reverence toward the United Nations have not attracted the scathing criticism they deserve. In chapter 3, the bishops become occasionally unrealistic and utopian, without advance criticism to rein them in. In one passage, they even describe, and seem to admire, surrender to a non-democratic enemy as a promotion of peace.

Uncertain Certainty

A close reading of the much-amended final text of chapter 2, the most debated section, shows that the bishops do approve of deterrence as did Pope John Paul II. By facing all the objections to deterrence, and by placing conditions on it, the bishops have in a sense given it its most sophisticated defense. It may, however, be too sophisticated. For the American bishops have tried to draw abstract conditions more narrowly than any Catholic body ever has before. As *The Economist* suggests, it is a defect connected with the métier of bishops, with their prime office, that, occupied as much as they are with universal moral principles, they may fall short just where concreteness is required. Bishops are tempted to be certain where no man can be certain, and to overestimate the weight (undoubtable though it be) of abstract principles in concrete actions. The clear principles of their final text do not much alter current realities.

Indeed, an instinct for this very circumstance from the first made some bishops eager to be ever more specific, ever more controversial and newsworthy, and above all and at any cost to seem vividly adversarial to the Reagan administration. When, for example, administration officials praised the third draft—homage one would have thought desirable—Archbishop Rembert Weakland of Milwaukee oddly said: "The White House co-opted the third draft before it was debated. That was unwise and impolitic." This must be the first pastoral in history adjusted in order to be publicly rejected. Such adjustments were mainly symbolic.

Whence came this itch to be adversarial, this prophet motive? Blame it in part on the Vietnam generation; most of the bishops are young—the bulk of them have been consecrated since 1965. Many now seem to be as unself-consciously on the Left as most used to be, before the Vatican Council, on the Right. Many blame Cardinal Spellman and his peers for not condemning the U.S. presence in Vietnam when so many other "prophets" were. But were these prophets true prophets? (Can it be said that the lot of the South Vietnamese is better in 1983 than it was in, say, 1973? Concentration camps abound today. Malnutrition is universal today. There were no boat people then. The ambiguous silence of the Catholic church then may now, in retrospect, seem to have been wise. Those of us who were then so morally certain about peace do not now look so morally pure.)

'Now We're Anti-Hannan'

In any case, referring to former paratrooper Archbishop Philip Hannan of New Orleans, who fought often alone and bravely against the Left at the Chicago meeting, and Bishop Thomas Gumbleton of Detroit, leader of the radical pacifists, a Midwestern bishop explained: "In the fifties, we were all Hannans. Now we're anti-Hannan and pro-Gumbleton." In short, the buzzword uniting "new moment" theology, a vivid personal conversion to "peacemaking," and left-wing politics is "prophecy." There may already be more self-proclaimed prophets among U.S. Catholic bishops

123

than in the entire Old Testament era and since the birth of Christ combined.

Furthermore, in a recent poll taken by the *National Catholic Register* among editors of the Catholic press, 67 per cent say they vote Democratic, 18 per cent Republican, 10 per cent other. Since 1965, the ranks of activist priests and nuns in new forms of ministry have swollen enormously, as many withdrew from parochial schools and ordinary parish work. Many such persons are available full-time to the religious arm of the activist Left. The clerocracy is thus hardly bipartisan, and for obvious reasons defines political issues in highly charged moral terms, while channeling religious sentiments into political action.

Thus, when the bishops promise to use their new pastoral for "education," one knows institutionally what to expect. One more propaganda blitz from the Left is on the way. Those who try to raise questions, face real difficulties, argue with genuine civility, and continue discussion even in disagreement will find the going rough. For those who think they speak with the tongues of prophets and believe that their politics is religious in inspiration can hardly help thinking any who oppose them immoral.

Against such circumstances, the actual text of the pastoral letter is a sure defense. If anyone should try to intimidate you with the authority of the bishops, take note of all that text's carefully stated principles, caveats, whereases, contingent judgments, and counterarguments. Any careful reader will discover massive evidences of the Vatican memo of January 18 and 19 in the text. Hold to them as to a rock. With the help of the public and the Vatican, the U.S. bishops have produced a valiant text.

Chapter 4

JUST AND UNJUST NEGOTIATIONS

One of the gravest moral dangers to the peace movement is an ancient temptation which has plagued Judaism and Christianity throughout their history. It is the temptation of the children of light—the temptation to turn one's back on the realities of flesh, ambiguity, and sin, in order to inhabit (in one's mind) a lightsome world of peace, love, and perfection. This temptation afflicted the Essenes, communities of the perfect, before the time of Christ, and it has tempted Christians from the days of the Gnostic rival religions. To demand too much of this poor world of sin is to dishonor Christianity, since Christians, while not being *of* this world are called to live out their vocations *in* it. Since *God* is Light and Love, Christians are mightily tempted to pretend to light and love prematurely on their own account. It is hard for them to learn, with Aristotle, that in the world of political action "one must be satisfied with a tincture of virtue"[1] and, with Christ, that the agony in the garden and the cross are our earthly lot. We will not share any premature fulfillment of the resurrection; to think so is presumption.

Nonetheless, the children of light extravagantly

trust in reason, morality, and love. They seek to make the world (at least in their own minds) into their own pretended image. C. S. Lewis once wrote that this temptation of romantic fulfillment is the deepest spiritual ocean of the West, compared to which the Reformation was but a ripple. He tried to distinguish between "mere Christianity," lowly Christianity, and such blissful visions of peace. Perhaps he knew from daily struggles against temptation (and against ravaging disease) how plain and humble Christian realism must be. He objected to pacifism—as did Reinhold Niebuhr—on such grounds.[2]

One sees this distinction even in the Gospels. Recall 1 John 4:20–21, in which John asks how we know that we love God. We do not know this by consulting the feelings in our heart, or by declaring that we do, or by trusting our own state of soul. We know that we love God by one test alone: whether we love our neighbor. And not just our "neighbor" in general, in the abstract, but the often disagreeable flesh-and blood persons we happen actually to *see* beside us. Every person is sometimes disagreeable to us, as we are to ourselves. Loving a real neighbor is as difficult as loving our self.

According to Professor Lapide, in the actual language of Jesus—Aramaic—the commandment to love God places "God" in the accusative case; God is truly worthy of love, though we do not see Him. But the commandment to love our neighbor places "neighbor" in the dative case; love of neighbor means *doing* something *for* our neighbor, *acting* in some way on his behalf. Thus, the Sermon on the Mount tells us that Christians are not Christians because they have pure opinions, or take noble public stands, or make lovely moral declarations—but if, and only if, they actually *do* things for their real neighbors: feed, clothe, visit them. "Blessed are the peacemakers," we are told. Not those who *speak* of peace, or *declare* their peacefulness, or aspire to peace, but those who *make* peace, the peace*makers*. Making peace is far more difficult than saying peace. Its accomplishment is to be judged in the external world, by deeds and consequences, not solely in the mental world of good intentions.

It is not so easy to be a peacemaker, especially (but not solely) in our own era. For the enemy we face, the Soviet Union, comes as close to incarnating within itself a kingdom of the lie, violence, and systemic aggression as has any regime in recorded history. Hear Solzhenitsyn's Nobel Lecture:

> Let us not forget that violence does not and cannot flourish by itself; it is inevitably intertwined with LYING. Between them there is the closest, the most profound and natural bond: nothing screens violence except lies, and the only way lies can hold out is by violence. Whoever has once announced violence as his METHOD must inexorably choose lying as his PRINCIPLE. At birth, violence behaves openly and even proudly. But as soon as it becomes stronger and firmly established, it senses the thinning of the air around it and cannot go on without befogging itself in lies, coating itself with lying's sugary oratory. It does not always or necessarily go straight for the gullet; usually it demands of its victims only allegiance to the lie, only complicity in the lie.[3]

Since the beginnings of Lenin's terror in 1923, Solzhenitsyn conservatively calculates that the rulers of the Soviet Union have murdered 65 million of their own citizens. Set *these* beside the 20 million deaths they are said to regret so deeply from the war against Hitler.

We are told that we should love our enemies, and some conclude (Bishop Walter Sullivan of Richmond said so in my own parish in the spring of 1983) that we must also love the Russians. As a Slav, I do not find this difficult at all. As the Japanese and the Germans were in my childhood dreaded enemies and as they today are perhaps our closest friends, so it is easy to imagine brotherhood between Russians and Americans. What stands athwart this possibility is not ill-will but the very real and powerful Leninist regime which throttles the Russian people. It is not difficult, either, to love individual members of that regime (whom fate has allowed me to meet from time to time). Still, one cannot avoid sensing the dreadful power of that regime over them—over their lives, their careers, their families, their words.

Making peace with that regime is all the more difficult because, in order to be true to itself, it *must* believe in its inexorable historical triumph over doomed regimes like ours; and in victory through struggle. Marxist-Leninists are, after all, not *Christian* Socialists, or *utopian* Socialists—for whom both Marx and Lenin taught the most intense scorn.

Such a regime believes in the efficacy of material power and in the decree of history which grounds its right to do whatever is necessary not only to prevail but to bury the foredoomed.

The struggle in which *both* the American people and the Russian people are engaged is against one of the most thoroughly brutal ideologies in human history. It is a struggle of the human spirit, primarily, but it is also a struggle of arms, which the Soviet regime intends to win, a struggle which is their primary, almost solitary, preoccupation. And "winning" means to them not necessarily by war but preferably by politics: by disinformation, lies, deceptions, demoralization, terror, intimidation and, at last, the supine surrender of the morally weak. Solzhenitsyn writes:

> There is a German proverb which runs *Mut verloren— alles verloren:* "When courage is lost, all is lost." There is another Latin one, according to which loss of reason is the true harbinger of destruction. But what happens to a society in which both these losses—the loss of courage and the loss of reason—intersect? This is the picture which I found the West presents today.[4]

Looked at from this perspective, a peace movement in the West which miscalculates the nature of the deadly struggle in which we are engaged commits itself to suicide. Worse than that, it cannot win by preemptive surrender the assurance that the Soviet regime as it now exists, or as it may yet exist in the hands of some new Machiavelli now unborn, will not plunge the world into nuclear war. Even were the United States to divest itself of nuclear arms, would China supinely surrender to the Soviets? Would world wars cease because the United States had foolishly unmanned itself? There is no such guarantee. On the contrary, absolute power unchecked would roam the world. The terrors of the present are not the worst the world has known or yet may know.

Consider the demand by the U.S. Catholic bishops that a nuclear deterrent is tolerable only on condition that arms control negotiations proceed successfully. What warrant is there for trusting negotiations? Regimes do not go to war because they lack solemn treaties of peace and arms control. On the contrary, virtually all wars contravene solemn agreements between regimes. Peace does not spring from negotiations. Regimes which do not want to share mutual peace and commerce arm themselves, no matter what arms control agreements they enter into. Thus, arms control negotiations are not always moral projects. They are sometimes hypocritical, deceptive, deadly. One needs to develop a morality of "just negotiations," even as there exists already a morality of the "just war." For during our lifetime alone there have already been many immoral and unjust arms control and nonaggression pacts.

Nothing is easier for an aggressive power than to mask its purposes through formal ceremonies which please and flatter their intended victims. Entering into such negotiations with false enthusiasm and silly hopes is no moral act, neither for self-deceived publics nor for the self-deceived individuals who participate in them.

Arms control negotiations with the Soviets may be useful. They may also be deadly. We lack a calculus of moral principles to help us to decide which is which. Certainly, negotiations entered into from passions of haste, anxiety, weakness, or fear are not likely to be moral. For successful negotiations, one must not have too great a passion to conclude. Especially with the Soviets, endurance is of the essence, since Communists are accomplished masters of winning through fatigue. The newspapers carried a story not long ago of a Soviet emissary returning to Moscow for a high award, merited by participating successfully in negotiations for eighteen years without concluding anything at all.

And one must not approach from weakness. Nor in fear.

Those who hold that history is ruthless and that force alone is its iron law can afford to wear a thousand costumes and to show a myriad of moods. Their underlying message in every mood is always the same: *"Surrender. Now or later. Superior force will do you in. History has so decreed."*

One must grasp the underlying spiritual power of Marxism-Leninism, if one is to dispel its grip. It draws millions like moths toward its distant glow of inevitability and fate. "The fate of the earth," Jonathan Schell writes; "the tide of history," Senator Christopher Dodd has cited. More and more Westerners speak the Marxist vulgate. It has become the spiritual language of our time.

That is why the real task of deterrence is better brought out by the French word, *dissuasion*. Even in English, dissuasion connotes the task more exactly: dissuading the Soviets from what they would otherwise feel obliged to do, simply in order to be faithful to themselves. For in their eyes, their regime is not evil but good (or, in any case, the only regime they have any prospect of having). To understand the Soviet regime exactly is not to be Manichean, as if it were the focus of all evil and the West purely good, but rather to be prudent. Illusions assist us not at all.

Seeing the many signs of moral decadence, loss of courage, and loss of will in the West, one cannot believe that the West is wholly good. Seeing the vast long suffering of the patient Russian people, seeing the nobility of so many courageous souls like Orlov, Scharansky, Sakharov, and others, one cannot believe that the Soviet Union is wholly evil. Of the West, Solzhenitsyn writes:

> In a state of psychological weakness, weapons even become a burden for the capitulating side. To defend oneself, one must also be ready to die; there is little such readiness in a society raised in the cult of material well-being. Nothing is left, in this case, but concessions, attempts to gain time, and betrayal. . . . But one must be blind in order not to see that the oceans no longer belong to the West, while the land under its domination keeps shrinking. The two so-called world wars (they were by far not on a world scale, not yet) constituted the internal self-destruction of the small progressive West which has thus prepared its own end. The next war (which does not have to be an atomic one; I do not believe it will be) may well bury Western civilization forever. . . . In the face of such a danger, with such historical values in your past, with such a high level of attained freedom and, apparently, of devotion to it, how is it possible to lose to such an extent the will to defend oneself?[5]

I do not believe that the West is as weak as Solzhenitsyn fears. In particular, I know that the American people, perhaps especially the religious, believing people of America, have not lost their will.

Sudden fear there is, appropriate and momentary. It will pass. For, gradually, the more each of us thinks about it, the more clearly each of us sees that dissuasion is our only sure defense, strength our only sure dissuader, and moral clarity the only long-range weapon able to penetrate a regime of lies.

The one reliable hope for the removal of the nuclear menace is a change in regimes within the Soviet Union. The fulfillment of such a hope may be a long time off, but it will come. For a regime built on lies slowly chokes itself. Even among thieves there must be honor.

For this we work and pray. In the meantime, we must dissuade the worst impulses of that regime from being realized. We do so only through unyielding and unbroken strength, strength of soul and strength of arms.

> He who dwells in the shelter of
>   the Most High,
> who abides in the shadow of the
>   Almighty,
> will say to the LORD, "My refuge and
>   my fortress;
>   my God, in whom I trust."
> For he will deliver you from the snare
>   of the fowler
> and from the deadly pestilence;
> he will cover you with his pinions,
>   and under his wings you will find
>   refuge;
>   his faithfulness is a shield and buckler.

Moral Clarity in the Nuclear Age

You will not fear the terror of the night,
  nor the arrow that flies by day,
nor the pestilence that stalks in darkness,
  nor the destruction that wastes at
    noonday.

—Psalm 91

NOTES

Author's Preface

1. Andrei Sakharov, "The Danger of Thermonuclear War," *Foreign Affairs* 61 (Summer 1983): 1015.

Chapter 1: Moral Clarity in the Nuclear Age

1. See Maritain, Appendix, "The Structure of Action," *Integral Humanism*, trans. Joseph W. Evans (New York: Scribner's, 1968), pp. 291–308. Addressing the Society of Jesus on February 27, 1982, John Paul II said: "As I said on 2 July 1980 in Rio de Janiero, priestly service 'if it is really to be faithful to itself, is essentially and *par excellence* spiritual. This must be even more emphasized in our times against the many tendencies to secularize the priest's work by reducing it to a purely philanthropic function. He is not a medical doctor, a social worker, a politician, or a trade unionist. In certain cases, no doubt, the priest can help, but in a supplementary fashion—as in the past priests have done so with remarkable success. Today, however, these services are admirably rendered by other members of society, whilst our service is always more precisely and specifically spiritual.' " (*Allocution of Pope John Paul II to Jesuit Provincial Superiors.*) In his follow-up Letter of March 25,

1982, to the entire Society of Jesus, Father Paolo Dezza applied the prescriptions of the Holy Father, while speaking of the recommendations presented by Pope Paul VI: "The second recommendation was not to confuse roles proper to priests with those proper to lay people. In the economic, social and political fields, the role of the priest is to educate toward justice and social commitment, and to encourage lay people to carry out their duties fully without replacing them in these. The priest's role is to indicate Christian principles concerning economic, social and political life; to denounce injustices, to exhort people to work with the improvement or reform of institutions, to 'expound the social doctrine of the Church, not so much as to find solutions for concrete social and political problems, which is the task of lay people, but to help them reflect on the principles which should guide the search for such solutions.'"

2. Walter M. Abbott, S.J., ed., *The Documents of Vatican II* (New York: America Press, 1966), fn. 2, p. 199.

3. Ibid., pp. 293–94.

4. Ibid., p. 291.

5. Ibid., p. 290.

6. Ibid., p. 293.

7. John Paul II, "World Day of Peace Message 1982," #12, *Origins* 11 (1982): 478.

8. Ibid.

9. See *Documents of Vatican II*, p. 244.

10. C. S. Lewis, "Why I Am Not a Pacifist," in *The Weight of Glory,* rev. ed. (New York: Macmillan, 1980), p. 44.

11. John Paul II, "Address to Scientists and Scholars," #4, *Origins* 10 (1982): 621.

12. See *Budget of the United States Government: Fiscal Year 1983* (Washington, D.C.: Office of Management and Budget, 1982), p. 3–33; and Caspar W. Weinberger, *Annual Report to Congress, Fiscal Year 1983*, pp. I–4, A–9.

13. *The Military Balance 1982-83* (London: International Institute for Strategic Studies, 1982), pp. 124–25.

14. Ibid., pp. 12–13. Note that the Soviet GNP is lower than that of the U.S.; but its costs, not least in salaries to military and military industries, are much lower.

15. U.S. Bureau of the Census, *The Statistical Abstract of the United States: 1981* (Washington, D.C.: U.S. Government Printing Office, 1981), p. 359.

16. See *Budget of the United States Government: Fiscal Year 1983*, p. 3–34; and "Welfare Need and Welfare Spending," *Backgrounder* #219 (Washington, D.C.: The Heritage Foundation, 1982).

17. Caspar W. Weinberger, *Annual Report to the Congress, Fiscal Year 1983*, p. A–9.

18. *The Challenge of Peace: God's Promise and Our Response* (Washington, D.C.: United States Catholic Conference, 1982), p. 70.

19. Quoted in ibid., p. 38.

20. Secretary of Defense Caspar Weinberger notes: "We have fewer nuclear warheads today than we had in 1967—not a handful fewer but thousands fewer." News Release No. 168–82, April 20, 1982, Office of Assistant Secretary of Defense (Public Affairs). In his report to congress on the fiscal year 1984 defense budget, Secretary Weinberger elaborated: "The number in our stockpile was one-third higher in 1967 than in 1980. Nor have we been accumulating more destructive weapons. The average number of kilotons per weapon has declined since the late 1950s, and the total number of megatons in our stockpile was four times as high in 1960 than in 1980. With the retirement of the Titans, this total will decline even further." *Annual Report to the Congress, Fiscal Year 1984*, p. 55. Although the exact number of nuclear warheads is classified, a careful student can deduce that the throwweight of the U.S. strategic missile force has declined by about one-half in the past decade-and-a-half.

21. The Soviet ICBM force currently numbers 1,398 missiles, compared to 1,052 for the U.S., and possesses greater aggregate throwweight than the U.S. missile force. The latest generation of Soviet missiles is more accurate than their American counterparts, and the smallest Soviet MIRVd warheads are almost twice as large as the largest U.S. MIRVd warheads. See *The Military Balance 1982–83*, pp. 112–13; and Committee on the Present Danger, *Has America Become Number 2?* (Washington, D.C., 1982), p. 16.

22. Admiral Thomas Hayward, the Chief of Naval Operations, testified before the Senate Armed Services Committee in 1979: "With respect to essential equivalence it is my view that without any question the Soviets will have a first-strike capability over the next few years. If that is not a loss of essential equivalence, I do not know what is. . . ." *Military Implications of the Treaty on the Limitation of Strategic Arms and Protocol Thereto*, Hearings, Senate Armed Services Committee, Part I, p. 177.

23. After chronicling the various unsuccessful efforts at arms control in this century, historian Barbara Tuchman says: "I have engaged in this long and dreary survey in order to show that control of war in the form of disarmament or limitation of arms has been a fruitless effort." Part of the reason why this is the case is suggested by the following observation by Salvador de Madariaga, chairman of the League of Nations Disarmament Commission and Disarmament Conference, in 1973, which Tuchman quotes: "The trouble with disarmament was (and still is) that the problem of war is tackled upside down and at the wrong end. . . . Nations don't distrust each other because they are armed; they are armed because they distrust each other. And therefore to want disarmament before a minimum of common agreement on fundamentals is as absurd as to want people to go undressed in winter." Barbara W. Tuchman, "The Alternative to Arms Control," *New York Times Magazine*, April 18, 1982, pp. 93, 98. See also Theodore

Notes

Draper, "How Not to Think About Nuclear War," *New York Review of Books*, July 15, 1982, pp. 35–43. "Once different weapons and even different weapons systems must be evaluated and balanced off against each other, negotiations inevitably degenerate into endlessly futile haggling sessions, brought to a close only by agreement on a crazy quilt of trade-offs and loopholes. Negotiations of this sort become more important for the mere consolation that the deadly antagonists are negotiating than for anything the negotiations may bring forth. . . . Short of abolishing all nuclear weapons forever and everywhere, deterrence is all we have" (p. 42).

24. Modernization of the Soviet ICBM force has focused on the SS-17, SS-18, and SS-19 missiles; during the last decade, over half of the Soviet silos have been rebuilt to house these weapons. See Department of Defense, *Soviet Military Power* (Washington, D.C.: U.S. Government Printing Office, 1981), p. 24. Of particular concern is the giant SS-18, which carries a payload large enough and accurate enough to threaten U.S. ICBMs in their silos. The SS-18, of which 308 have been deployed, dwarfs the proposed MX: it is 120 feet high, 10 feet in diameter, has a throwweight of 16,000 pounds, and can carry up to 10 warheads. By comparison, the MX, which cannot be deployed before 1986, is 72 feet in length, about 8 feet in diameter, possesses a throwweight of about 8,000 pounds, and can carry 6 to 10 warheads. The SS-19 is comparable in these respects to the MX. See *The Military Balance 1982–83*, p. 113 and Michael B. Donley, ed., *The SALT Handbook* (Washington, D.C.: The Heritage Foundation, 1979), pp. 62, 75. The Committee on the Present Danger notes that "in only the last five years, the number of deployed Soviet IRBM [Intermediate Range Ballistic Missile] warheads targeted on NATO—Europe and Asia—has more than doubled." *Has America Become No. 2?*, p. 21. The principal threat is the Soviet SS-20: "The SS-20, with three MIRVs per missile and significant improvements in sur-

vivability, mobility, responsiveness, and accuracy, is a far more capable weapon than the older SS-4 and SS-5 missiles . . . . [it] can cover the entire European theatre and provide significant coverage of other areas." Organization of the Joint Chiefs of Staff, *United States Military Posture for FY 1983*, p. 27.

25. Charles Mohr, "Drop in U.S. Arms Spurs Debate on Military Policy," *New York Times*, October 24, 1982, p. 56. For spending on nuclear forces as a percentage of the military budget for 1962 to 1982, see Kevin N. Lewis, *The Economics of SALT Revisited* (Santa Monica, Calif.: Rand Corp., 1979), p. 10, and Caspar W. Weinberger, *Annual Report to Congress, Fiscal Year 1983*, p. A–1.

26. For the number of U.S. military personnel in NATO, see *Defense/81*, Special Almanac Issue (September 1981): 22. The cost of the U.S. commitment to NATO is given in the remarks of Senator Ted Stevens on the continuing appropriations legislation for fiscal year 1983. See U.S. Congress, Senate, *Congressional Record*, 97th Cong., 2d. sess., December 16, 1982, 149, pt. 3: S15138. The budget figure for nuclear forces includes both those over which the Department of Defense has jurisdictions and those which the Department of Energy supervises, and covers all personnel, operation and maintenance, and warhead procurement costs, strategic as well as tactical/theater.

27. See *The Military Balance 1982–83*, pp. 112–13, 140; and *Soviet Military Power*, pp. 55–56. The data supplied by these sources indicate that about 62 per cent of U.S. strategic warheads are on systems with an initial operational capability prior to 1972, whereas 70 per cent of Soviet strategic warheads are on systems initially deployed since 1977

28. *The Military Balance 1982–83*, pp. 132-33. For figures on the U.S. Navy see *Annual Report to Congress, Fiscal Year 1983*, p. III–20. For the Soviet Navy, see *Soviet Military Power*, p. 40. Both sets of figures include attack submarines, major surface combat vessels and minor surface comba-

tants (corvettes, patrol craft, minesweepers, amphibious ships, and support craft). The U.S. figure as given in the *Report to Congress* does not include ballistic missile submarines; the Soviet figure does. Adding this figure (32) to the U.S. count gives 546 ships.

29. See the analysis by Edward N. Luttwak, "How to Think About Nuclear War," *Commentary* 74 (August 1982): 21–28.

30. "Without the Bomb," *The Economist* (July 31, 1982): 11–12.

31. See Derek Leebaert, letter to the Editor, *New York Times*, April 18, 1982.

Chapter 2: The Geopolitical Situation: A View from Europe

1. Alexander Solzhenitsyn, *Warning to the West* (New York: Farrar, Straus, and Giroux, 1976), pp. 76–77.

2. Andrei Sakharov, "The Danger of Thermonuclear War," *Foreign Affairs* 61 (Summer 1983): 1010.

3. Ralph Lerner, "Commerce and Character: The Anglo-American as New-Model Man," *William and Mary Quarterly* 36 (January 1979): 5; reprinted in Michael Novak, ed., *Liberation South, Liberation North* (Washington, D.C.: American Enterprise Institute, 1981).

4. Press conference of March 21, 1962, in *Public Papers of the Presidents of the United States: John F. Kennedy, 1961*, 3 vols. (Washington, D.C.: U.S. Government Printing Office, 1963), II: 259; and Inaugural Address, ibid., I: 1–2.

5. Testimony of Hon. David A. Stockman, Director, Office of Management and Budget, before the Joint Economic Committee, U.S. Congress, May 4, 1983. Nuclear weapons expenditures are computed from the National Defense Budget Estimates published annually by the Office of the Assistant Secretary of Defense (Comptroller).

6. See Albert Wohlstetter, "Bishops, Statesmen and Other Strategists on the Bombing of Innocents," *Commentary* 65 (June 1983): 15–35.

7. J. Bryan Hehir, for example, contends that "counterforce strategy is subject to the criticism that it makes nuclear war 'thinkable,' increasing the probability of wars being started with such weapons or of such weapons being employed because they are controllable, with one side or both tempted to escalate the conflict to an 'all-out' nuclear exchange." "The Catholic Church and the Arms Race," *Worldview* (July–August 1978): 15.

8. "We must lay down our arms, relinquish sovereignty, and found a political system for the peaceful settlement of international disputes. . . . Since the goal would be a nonviolent world, the actions of this endeavor would be nonviolent. . . . With the world itself at stake, all differences would by definition be 'internal' differences, to be resolved on the basis of respect for those with whom one disagreed." Jonathan Schell, *The Fate of the Earth* (New York: Avon Books, 1982), pp. 226, 229. See also Walter Berns, "The New Pacifism and World Government," *National Review* (May 27, 1983): 613–20.

9. The bishops' pastoral letter states: "Just as the nation-state was a step in the evolution of government at a time when expanding trade and new weapons technologies made the feudal system inadequate to manage conflicts and provide security, so we are now entering an era of new, global interdependencies requiring global systems of governance to manage the resulting conflicts and ensure our common security. . . . As we shall indicate below, the United Nations should be particularly considered in this effort." "The Challenge of Peace: God's Promise and Our Response," *Origins* (May 19, 1983): 23.

10. Andrei Sakharov observes: "I know that pacifist sentiments are very strong in the West. I deeply sympathize with people's yearning for peace, for a solution to world problems by peaceful means; I share those aspirations

fully. But, at the same time, I am certain that it is absolutely necessary to be mindful of the specific political, military, and strategic realities of the present day and to do so objectively without making any sort of allowances for either side; this also means that one should not proceed from an a priori assumption of any special peace-loving nature in the socialist countries due to their supposed progressiveness or the horrors and losses they have experienced in war. Objective reality is much more complicated and far from anything so simple. People both in the socialist and the Western countries have a passionate inward aspiration for peace. This is an extremely important factor, but, I repeat, itself alone does not exclude the possibility of a tragic outcome." "The Danger of Thermonuclear War," p. 1011. See the report on the efforts of Sergei Batovrin to found a Soviet peace movement, in the *New York Times*, February 21, 1983. Mr. Batovrin's efforts have resulted in his internment in a Moscow psychiatric hospital; his group continues to be subject to severe harassment by Soviet authorities. Thus, our problem lies not with the Russian people—who may be presumed to desire peace as ardently as their Western counterparts—but with the Soviet regime.

Chapter 3: Rescued from Disaster: The Bishops Speak Out

1. The full text is printed in *Origins* (April 7, 1983): 691–95. (Published by the N.C. News Service, 1312 Massachusetts Avenue, N.W., Washington, D.C. 20005.)

Chapter 4: Just and Unjust Negotiations

1. *Nichomachean Ethics* 1179b20.
2. See Ronald H. Stone, *Reinhold Niebuhr: Prophet to Politicians* (Nashville, Tenn.: Abingdon Press, 1972), pp. 73–79.

3. Alexander Solzhenitsyn, *Nobel Lecture* (New York: Farrar, Straus and Giroux, 1972), pp. 32–33.

4. Idem, *Warning to the West* (New York: Farrar, Straus and Giroux, 1976), pp. 126–27. Solzhenitsyn's estimates of 65 million political killings may be found in Edward E. Ericson, Jr., *Solzhenitsyn: The Moral Vision* (Grand Rapids, Mich.: William B. Eerdmans, 1980), p. 151.

5. Idem, *A World Split Apart* (New York: Harper and Row, 1978), pp. 45–47.